Obento
Supreme

おべんとう

D1615467

Ayako **Fukunaga**

Kyoko **Kusumoto**

Jacqueline **Brown**

Anne **Fisher**

Jean **Swinyard**

NELSON
CENGAGE Learning™

Australia · Canada · Mexico · New Zealand · Singapore · Spain · United Kingdom · United States

Obento Supreme
1st Edition

Editor: Craig Metcher
Project editor: Craig Metcher
Publishing editor: Olive McRae
Senior designer: Sue Dani
Text designers: Sue Dani and Yuri Tanabe
Text illustrators: Yuko Fujita, U-suke, Kae Sato-Goodsell, Tracie Grimwood, Nathan Jurevicius, Chris Lynch, Pat Reynolds and John Canty
Cover designer Sue Dani
Cover photographer: Brent Parker-Jones Photography
Internal photography: Brent Parker-Jones Photography
Production controller: Hanako Smith
Reprint: Jess Lovell
Typeset in DFP Kyokasho W3 11/19pt by Yuri Tanabe

Any URLs contained in this publication were checked for currency during the production process. Note, however, that the publisher cannot vouch for the ongoing currency of URLs.

Acknowledgements
The Publisher would like to credit or acknowledge the following sources for photographs: Jacqueline Brown, p. 159 top left; Ayako Fukunaga, pp. 118, 119, 127 top; Getty Images/AFP by YOSHIKAZU TSUNO, p. 159 centre right & centre bottom /AFP, pp. 126, top left, 127 bottom left & right, 159 bottom left, 159 centre (comic) /DAJ, p. 47 centre right /Hideki Matsui, p. 127 top right /Kosuke Kitajima, p. 130 (swimmer) /Taxi, pp. 47 centre right, bottom left /Time & Life Pictures by Anthony Verde, p. 159 centre left; Istockphotos.com, pp. 37 centre left, 91 top left & centre /Bart Parren, p. 25 top left /Carli Schultz, p. 91 top right /Diane Diederich, p. 144 /Edyta Pawtowska, p. 143 /Holger Feroudj, p. 91 bottom right /Jon Patton, p. 91 centre bottom /Marisa Allegra, p. 47 top left /Michael Chen, p. 91 centre left /Norah Scalin, p. 47, centre left /Oleg Prikhodko, p. 104 /Perry Wang, p. 102 bottom /Philip Dyer, p. 65 bottom right /Richard Scherzinger, p. 65 centre right /Ryan Tacay, p. 91 bottom left; photolibrary.com/Creatas, pp. 49 top; 159 centre (couple); Photos.com, pp. 65 top right, right; Bruce Postle, p. 126 top right; Courtesy of Toraya Confectionery Ltd, from Flowers and Wagashi, p. 90.

Kana-chan design and production team:
Anita Simadibrata, Concept, character design, graphic & audio production
Andrew Lawton, Flash programming and graphic production
Dylan Davis, Project manager

Cengage Learning would like to thank the following models and voice actors for participating in the Obento Supreme project: Aya Suganuma, Kensuke Kumagai, Yuko Fujita, Kazuo Burgess, Ami Enomoto, Takashi Takiguchi, Azumi Kobayashi, Ai Nagoya, Arata Higa, Ying Hua, Chika Hashimoto, Soo-Joo Yoo, Michinao Hattori, Yumiko Seotani, Katsuya Mori, Naho Fujimoto, Rina Satoh, Risa Fukuwa, Rui Nakanishi, Haru Fujikawa, Yoshiyuki Fujiu, Maki Yasuhara, Fukari Sato.

For product information and technology assistance, in Australia call **1300 790 853**; in New Zealand call **0800 449 725**

For permission to use material from this text or product, please email **aust.permissions@cengage.com**

National Library of Australia Cataloguing-in-Publication Data
Obento Supreme.
For secondary school students
ISBN 978 0 17 012964 0

1. Japanese language - Textbooks for foreign speakers-English. 2. Japanese language - Writing - Textbooks. 3. Japan - Social life and customs. I. Fisher, Anne. (Series: Obento :2)
495.682421

Cengage Learning Australia
Level 7, 80 Dorcas Street
South Melbourne, Victoria Australia 3205

Cengage Learning New Zealand
Unit 4B Rosedale Office Park
331 Rosedale Road, Albany, North Shore 0632, NZ

For learning solutions, visit **cengage.com.au**

Printed in China by China Translation & Printing Services.
10 11 12 13 14 15 16 17 16 15 14 13

Welcome

Welcome to *Obento Supreme*, the second book in the *Obento* series.

This book contains 12 units introducing a variety of interesting topics relevant to the everyday world of students. These range from fashion and media to home stay in Japan. You will learn to communicate with Japanese students your own age, talking about your home life and your leisure activities as well as your school life and the world of part-time work, and to function in the Japanese speaking world.

As with all the books in the *Obento* series, you are encouraged to use every aspect of language learning to communicate in Japanese. Within each of the units in this book you will find sentence patterns and vocabulary and exercises that equip you well for communicating in Japanese. But you don't need to understand everything you hear or read – there are often situations where guesswork and gestures play an important part in conversation.

The sections of this book differ from the first book, *Obento Deluxe*. The first page of each unit introduces the theme and outlines what you can expect to achieve on completion of the unit. It is both an introduction and a summary of the unit.

The first section of the unit covers a variety of text types from letters and e-mails to phone conversations and recounts. This section is the same as いただきます in *Obento Deluxe*. It introduces the unit theme using key language supported by visual material and audio CDs.

The れんしゅう section gives an example of the sentence patterns introduced in the unit. It offers speaking and listening practice of the key elements and replaces the どんなあじ section of *Obento Deluxe*. The patterns are recorded on CD to give you maximum practice.

In the かんじ section, the new kanji for the unit are introduced. Each kanji is shown with its stroke order, readings as appropriate, English meaning and example words or phrases. Remember that writing takes practice, practice and more practice. That's the way Japanese students learn it and you will perfect it the same way.

ぶんぽう introduces the grammar through example sentences. The たんご list gives you the main vocabulary for the unit although each reading passage will have its own list of extra words as well.

The ぶんぽうプラス section gives detailed explanations of the grammar points introduced in each unit. It provides extra examples and draws attention to the tricky aspects of the sentence patterns introduced.

The エクストラ section gives you more reading practice and some examples of texts you can produce yourself, such as e-mails, invitations and letters. Once you have practised the sentence patterns through drills, reading will reinforce the grammar and help you remember the vocabulary. The more you read, the more confident you will become in using the new language patterns. This section also gives you cultural information about Japan, thereby expanding your understanding of the Japanese people. Cultural knowledge is just as important as language in helping you to communicate.

In addition to the above features *Obento Supreme* is supported by speaking wordlists, interactive activities, a mobile phone game, kanji flashcards, a wordfinder and the *Obento* website, which can be found at www.obento.com.au.

Please use this book and its components to enjoy your study of the Japanese people and their language.

この本で 日本語の べんきょうを
たのしんでください。

contents

四

Unit 7 79
いただきます！

asking what someone is doing at the moment and responding

asking and saying how many general items you want

asking and saying how many items (in glasses or cups) you want

recognising and using common expressions at restaurants

kanji: 食，飲，行，買，大，小，安，高

Unit 9 105
まっすぐ　行きます

asking where something is

giving directions

saying when/if you do something and what happens next

joining two or more sets of actions

using the structure てから

asking how long it takes to go somewhere or to do something and responding

kanji: 右，左，入，出，南，北，西，東

Yoshi

Unit 11 131
アルバイト

talking about things you do in non-sequential order

saying what you want to become

comparing two things and giving your opinion

reading and writing a modified curriculum vitae in Japanese

preparing for a job interview in Japanese

participating in a job interview

reading and writing a job application letter in Japanese

kanji: 語，英，家，友，会，社，間，町

Unit 8 93
こうかん
りゅうがくせい

asking for and giving permission to do something

refusing permission to do something

asking someone to do something for you and responding when asked

asking the reason why and responding when asked

kanji: 私，男，女，書，見，聞，父，母

Unit 10 117
スポーツヒーロー

making the dictionary form of verbs

saying that you like or dislike doing things

saying that someone is good at or not good at doing something

saying that you can, cannot, could or could not do something

conducting an interview in Japanese

kanji: 毎，今，週，先，来，住，好，名

Unit 12 145
メディア

asking and saying what someone will try doing

asking and saying what someone is doing while doing something else

asking and saying what you have or have not done

recognising and using the plain negative form of present and past tense verbs

revising the て form and the plain form of verbs

recognising casual speech

recognising some ending particles

kanji: 新，読，電，車，外，国，話，々

menu

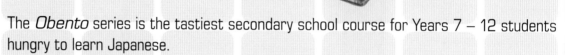

The *Obento* series is the tastiest secondary school course for Years 7 – 12 students hungry to learn Japanese.

Obento Supreme is designed to cover two years of intermediate Japanese language study. It forms a seamless transition between Obento Deluxe and Obento Senior.

Obento Supreme has four components:

1 The **Student Book**, which consists of 12 units. The sections marked with a CD icon are recorded on the Teacher Audio CDs. At the back of the Student Book you can find wordlists and additional information.

2 The **Workbook**, which consolidates the material in the Student Book. It also contains listening material marked by a CD icon. This listening material can be found on the Teacher Audio CDs. At the back of the Workbook you can find kanji flashcards and a CD-ROM containing interactive activities similar to the れんしゅう section of the Student Book, and a speaking wordfinder.

3 The **Teacher Audio CDs**, which contain audio recordings for all the text marked with a CD icon in the Student Book, Workbook and Teacher Resource Book. The Teacher Audio CDs, which are sold separately, can be networked or copied within your school by yourself and your students.

4 The **Teacher Resource Book (TRB)**, which contains the Blackline Masters (BLMs) grouped by unit. In the inside back cover there is a CD-ROM. On this CD-ROM you will find detailed teacher notes and solutions to the Workbook and BLM activities. Purchase one TRB for you and your colleagues to use.

+

- A **free** mobile phone game to practise hiragana and katakana inside the back cover of the Student Book.
- The **Obento Website**, which contains interactive activities and additional information to support teachers, students and parents. Visit **www.obento.com.au** or ask your sales representative for a CD-ROM to network on your intranet.

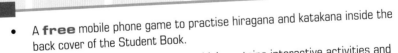

01

ゆきさんのカラオケパーティー

In this unit, you will learn to:

ask and tell time

ask and say what time you do something

ask and say when you do something

ask and say where you do activities

invite someone to do something and respond

recognise and write the kanji characters: 何 , 時 , 分 , 半

In this unit, you will learn about:

grammatical concepts which operate across languages

the Japanese way of expressing an invitation

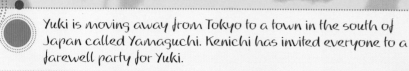

Yuki is moving away from Tokyo to a town in the south of Japan called Yamaguchi. Kenichi has invited everyone to a farewell party for Yuki.

月曜日、がっこうの　あとで

Kenichi: ちえこさん、らいしゅうの　土曜日は　ひまですか。

Chieko: らいしゅうの　土曜日？　ひまですよ。

K: 土曜日は　ゆきさんの　さようならパーティーです。
パーティーに　きませんか。

C: えっ！　さようならパーティー？

K: はい。ゆきさんは　山口に　ひっこしを　します。

C: えっ！　いつですか。

K: らい月です。

C: えー？　さびしい。さようならパーティーは　何時ですか。

K: ごご　一時半です。

C: どこで　パーティーを　しますか。

K: カラオケ「ロックタイム」です。

C: わあ！　うたが　だいすき！　たのしみです。

Are you free?

I've got free time.

to move house

I will miss her.

I can't wait/I'm looking forward to it.

えきで

Chieko: みきさん、ゆきさんの　カラオケパーティーに　いきますか。

Miki: はい、しんごくんと　いきます。

C: 何で　いきますか。

M: でんしゃで　いきます。ちえこさんも　いっしょに　いきませんか。

C: いいですね。何時に　いきましょうか。

M: 一時五分に　えきで　あいましょう。

together

ゆきさんの
カラオケさようならパーティーに
きませんか。

ゆきさんは　山口に　ひっこしを　します。

いっしょに　うたを　うたいましょう。

ばしょ：カラオケ「ロックタイム」

時かん：3月15日（土曜日）ごご1時半

けんいちより

01

二

Questions

1 What does Kenichi ask Chieko on Monday?
2 What does Kenichi have planned?
3 When and where will this take place?
4 Who else is going?
5 How will they get there?
6 What does Miki suggest they do at 1.05 pm?

place
time
from Kenichi

2

れんしゅう

01 Asking and telling time

一 何時ですか。
　八時です。
二 何時ですか。
　いま　ごぜん　十時半です。
三 何時ですか。
　いま　ごご　三時五分です。
四 パーティーは　何時ですか。
　パーティーは　ごご　七時十分まえです。

02 Asking and saying what time you do an activity

一 何時に　バスに　のりますか。
　八時に　のります。
二 何時に　でかけましょうか。
　ごぜん　十時半に　でかけましょう。
三 何時に　うちに　きますか。
　きょう、ごご　三時五分に　いきます。

01

三

れんしゅう

03 Asking and saying when you do an activity

一　みきさん、いつ　しゅくだいを　しますか。
　　あした　します。

二　いつ　プレゼントを　かいましょうか。
　　らいしゅう　かいましょう。

三　いつ　コンサートに　いきますか。
　　らい月　いきます。

四　いつ　日本に　いきますか。
　　ことし　いきます。

04 Asking and saying where you do an activity

一　どこで　パーティーを　しますか。
　　ともだちの　うちで　します。

二　どこで　ひるごはんを　たべましょうか。
　　レストランで　たべましょう。

三　どこで　ボートに　のりましたか。
　　うみで　ボートに　のりました。

05 Inviting someone to do something and responding

一　あした　ぼくの　うちに　きませんか。
　　はい、いきます。

二　いっしょに　うたを　うたいませんか。
　　はい、うたいましょう。

三　コーラを　のみませんか。
　　すみません。コーラは　ちょっと…。

01

四

4

漢字
かんじ

These are the kanji and their readings introduced in this unit.

 なに／なん what

 何

Two people are saying 'What's in the box?'

ノ	イ	仁	仁	仞	伺	何

何を　しましょうか。→　なにを　しましょうか。→　What shall we do?

何時　→　なんじ　→　What time?

何曜日　→　なんようび　→　What day of the week?

何月何日　→　なんがつなんにち　→　What month, what date?

とき／ジ o'clock

時

Measuring time with a sun dial.

l	⊓	日	日	日⁻	日⁺	旪	旪
時	時						

三時　→　さんじ　→　3 o'clock

四時に　→　よじに　→　at 4 o'clock

いま　六時です。→　いま　ろくじです。→　It is 6 o'clock now.

時々　→　ときどき　→　sometimes

フン／プン minute

分

In the clock, there is a minute man pointing to the minutes.

ノ	八	分	分	

十五分　→　じゅうごふん　→　15 minutes

二十分　→　にじゅっぷん　→　20 minutes

三時五分まえに　→　さんじごふんまえに　→　at five to three

二時十分です。→　にじじゅっぷんです。→　It is 2.10.

ハン half

半

A karate black belt chopping three boards by hand and breaking them exactly in half. He calls out 'han!'

、	ヽ	⦁⦁	⸱⸱	半	

一時半　→　いちじはん　→　1.30

七時半に　→　しちじはんに　→　at 7.30

いま　十時半です。→　いま　じゅうじはんです。→　It is now 10.30.

五時半に　いきます。→　ごじはんに　いきます。→　I will go at 5.30.

01

五

Asking the time

いま　何時ですか。
What time is it now?

パーティーは　何時ですか。
What time is the party?

Telling the time

いま　ごぜん　二時十五分です。
It is 2:15 am now.

パーティーは　ごご　七時十五分まえです。
The party is at a quarter to 8 pm.

Asking what time you do an activity

何時に　ともだちに　あいますか。
What time will you meet your friend?

Saying what time you do an activity

一時に　ともだちに　あいます。
At 1 o'clock, I will meet my friend.

Asking when you do an activity

いつ　えいがに　いきますか。
When will you go to the movies?

Saying when you do an activity

あした　えいがに　いきます。
I will go to the movies tomorrow.

Asking where you do an activity

どこで　ともだちに　あいますか。
Where will you meet your friend?

Responding

がっこうで　ともだちに　あいます。
I will meet my friend at school.

Suggestions

たべましょうか。	Shall we eat?
のみましょうか。	Shall we drink?
ききましょうか。	Shall we listen?
みましょう。	Let's look.
しましょう。	Let's do.
のりましょう。	Let's ride.
とりましょう。	Let's take (photos).
でかけましょう。	Let's go out.

Invitations

あいませんか。	Won't you meet?
いきませんか。	Won't you go?
よみませんか。	Won't you read?
かきませんか。	Won't you write?
かいませんか。	Won't you buy?
うたいませんか。	Won't you sing?
べんきょうしませんか。	Won't you study?

Responding

はい、…ましょう。
Yes, let's …

すみません。〜は　ちょっと…。
Sorry, I am not really keen on …

01

六

たんご

Time (o'clock)

ごぜん	一時	いちじ	1 o'clock	am
ごご	二時	にじ	2 o'clock	pm
	三時	さんじ	3 o'clock	
	四時	よじ	4 o'clock	
	五時	ごじ	5 o'clock	
	六時	ろくじ	6 o'clock	
	七時	しちじ	7 o'clock	
	八時	はちじ	8 o'clock	
	九時	くじ	9 o'clock	
	十時	じゅうじ	10 o'clock	
	十一時	じゅういちじ	11 o'clock	
	十二時	じゅうにじ	12 o'clock	

Places

うみ		beach
えいがかん		movie theatre
えき		station
がっこう		school
きっさてん		coffee shop
こうえん		park
としょかん		library
ともだちの	うち	a friend's house
まち		town/city
みせ		shop
レストラン		restaurant
やま		mountains

Time (half past)

一時半	いちじはん	half past one
二時半	にじはん	half past two

Time (minutes)

九時十五分	くじじゅうごふん	9.15		
九時二十五分	くじにじゅうごふん	9.25		
九時三十五分	くじさんじゅうごふん	9.35	十時二十五分まえ	25 to 10:00
九時四十五分	くじよんじゅうごふん	9.45	十時十五分まえ	15 to 10:00
九時五十五分	くじごじゅうごふん	9.55	十時五分まえ	5 to 10:00
九時十分	くじじゅっぷん	9.10		
九時二十分	くじにじゅっぷん	9.20		
九時三十分	くじさんじゅっぷん	9.30	九時半	half past 9
九時四十分	くじよんじゅっぷん	9.40	十時二十分まえ	20 to 10:00
九時五十分	くじごじゅっぷん	9.50	十時十分まえ	10 to 10:00

Time words

Past		Present		Future	
きのう	yesterday	きょう	today	あした	tomorrow
せんしゅう	last week	こんしゅう	this week	らいしゅう	next week
せん月	last month	こん月	this month	らい月	next month
きょねん	last year	ことし	this year	らいねん	next year

01

七

7

文法
ぶんぽう Plus

おかしいなあ！ A puzzling question

Look at this invitation:

あした ぼくの うちに きませんか。(Won't you come to my house tomorrow?)
はい、いきます。(Yes, I'll go.)

Did you notice that the invitation uses the verb きませんか but the response is 「はい、いきます」? In English, we usually say, 'Would you like to come to my house?' and the reply is 'Yes, I would like to come'. But it is more logical to answer 'Yes, I will go' so as to show you are going to someone else's house.

Particle panic!

When do you use で, に, と and を?

で
Means of transport
でんしゃで いきました。

Places where you did something
としょかんで よみました。

に
Places you went to
としょかんに いきました。

Specific times when you do things
二時に いきましょう。

と
Doing something with someone or with a pet
ともだちと でかけました。
いぬと あそびました。

Something you do/did

ほん　よみます
えいが　みます
すし　たべます
コーラ　のみます
てがみ　かきます
テニス　します
CD　ききました
プレゼント　かいました

を

べんりな ヒント Handy hints!

In both English and Japanese, building a long sentence is like lining up blocks of information, Look at this example:

Yuki → went → to the beach → with her friend by train → on Sunday .

ゆきさんは → 日曜日に → ともだちと でんしゃで → うみに → いきました。

Family tree

If you want to say that you went somewhere with your own family, you sound more educated and sophisticated if you use humble family terms. Compare the humble terms (used to talk about your own family) and the polite terms (used to talk about someone else's family). When talking directly to your own family use polite terms.

Someone else's family (polite terms)

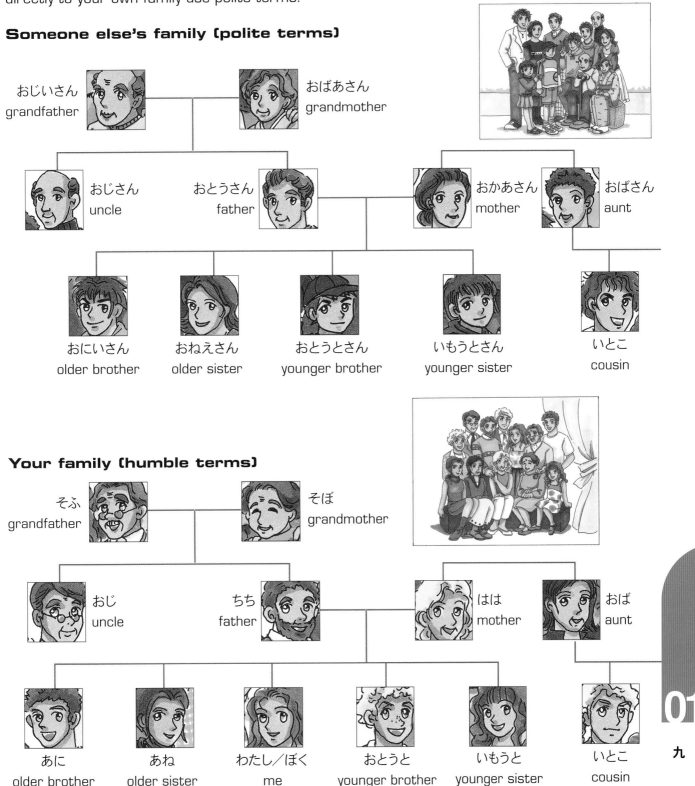

おじいさん
grandfather

おばあさん
grandmother

おじさん
uncle

おとうさん
father

おかあさん
mother

おばさん
aunt

おにいさん
older brother

おねえさん
older sister

おとうとさん
younger brother

いもうとさん
younger sister

いとこ
cousin

Your family (humble terms)

そふ
grandfather

そぼ
grandmother

おじ
uncle

ちち
father

はは
mother

おば
aunt

あに
older brother

あね
older sister

わたし／ぼく
me

おとうと
younger brother

いもうと
younger sister

いとこ
cousin

01

九

パーティーを　しませんか

カードを　つくりましょう

二月十九日は　わたしの
たんじょうびです。
たんじょうびパーティーに　きませんか。
すしパーティーです。
すしの　りょうりコンテストを　します。
そして、たくさん　たべます。

ばしょ：わたしの　うち
　時かん：2月21日（土曜日）ごご2時
　へんじは　金曜日まで

たのしみに　しています。

みかより

ニュー　イヤー　パーティー

ニュー　イヤー　パーティーに　きませんか。
おもしろい　ゲームを　しましょう。
一月四日、十二時に
わたしの　うちに　きてください。

ちえこ　より

ティー　パーティー

ティー　パーティーを　しましょう。
おいしい　ケーキを　たべませんか。
5月16日3時に　わたしの　うちで

ゆき　より

クリーン　アップ　ジャパン

五月二十日は　クリーン　アップ　ジャパン　デーです。
みんなで　かわの　そうじを　しましょう。

いつ？：　　五月二十日
何時？：　　ひる休みの　あとで
どこ？：　　がっこうで

みんなに　アイスクリームを　プレゼントします。
ぜひ、きてね。まってます！

せんせいより

ロック　コンサート

ぼくの　ロックバンド「オゾン」が
コンサートを　します。
「オゾン」の　おんがくを
きいてください。

ばしょ：うめだ　こうえん
日時：4月24日（日曜日）ごご5時

たかし　より

オゾンは
ぜったい
すごいゼ！

まってるヨ

けんくんです。

ゆうです。

たかしです。

エクストラ

Here are some useful expressions for invitations.
Listen to the CD and repeat what you hear.

Polite

～しませんか。	Won't you do ... ?
～しましょう。	Let's do ....
たのしみに　しています。	I am looking forward to it!
きてください。	Please come.

ばしょ	place/venue
時かん	time
日時	date and time
もってくるもの	things to bring
へんじは　金曜日まで。	RSVP by Friday.

すごい。	It is amazing.
とても　たのしいよ。	It will be a lot of fun.
ぜひ　きてね。	You must come!
わすれないで！	Don't forget!
でんわ　してね！	Call me!
へんじ　かいてね！	Write me a reply!
E メールしてね。	Send me an e-mail.
まってます／まってるよ。	I am waiting!

Casual

01

＋
—

スペースワールドに　いきましょう！

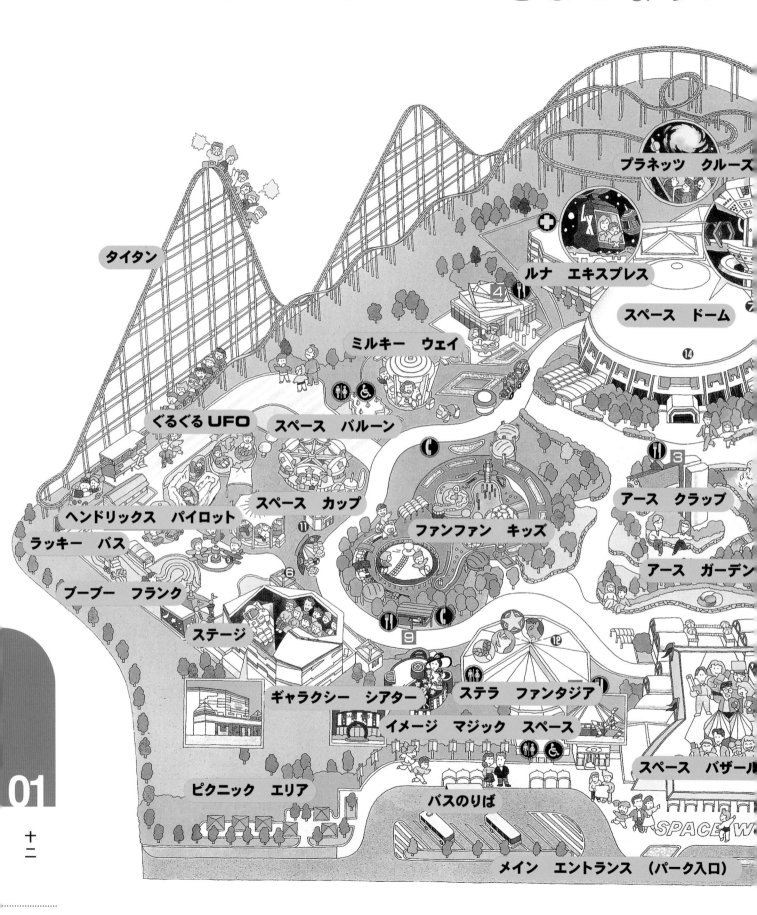

タイタン

プラネッツ　クルーズ

ルナ　エキスプレス

スペース　ドーム

ミルキー　ウェイ

ぐるぐる UFO

スペース　バルーン

ヘンドリックス　パイロット

スペース　カップ

ファンファン　キッズ

アース　クラブ

ラッキー　バス

ブーブー　フランク

アース　ガーデン

ステージ

ギャラクシー　シアター

ステラ　ファンタジア

イメージ　マジック　スペース

スペース　バザール

ピクニック　エリア

バスのりば

メイン　エントランス　（パーク入口）

Look for the following places in the Space World Guide.
As you find the places, read them aloud in Japanese.

Main Entrance	Star Shaker	The Stage	Clipper
Galaxy Theatre	Space Camp	Space Cup	Free Fall
Super Planet	Milky Way	Cosmo Fighter	Stellar Fantasia
Black Hole Scramble	Lunar Express	Space Lodge	Cosmo Pier
	Lucky Bus	Picnic Area	Taxi Stand
	Fun Fun Kids	Planet Cruise	Image Magic Space
	Earth Club	Lunar Swing	Cosmic Eye
		Space Balloon	Vroom Vroom Frank
		Space Dome	Titan
		Earth Garden	Hendrix Pilot
		Venus	Spinning UFO
		Bus Stop	Space Coaster
			Space Bazaar
			Discovery Square

ブラック　ホール　スクランブル

スモ　ピア

スター　シェイカー

フリー　フォール

スーパー　プラネット

コスモ　ファイター

スペース　コースター

ディスカバリー　スクエア

クリッパー

コズミック　アイ

スペース　ロッジ

ルナ　スウィング

スペース　キャンプ

タクシーのりば

ヴィーナス

すごろくをしませんか。

スタート

Say that you will go to school at 7:00 am.

Say that you will do your homework tomorrow.

Read the clock face.

Name four activities that you do on the weekend.

Fill in the missing particles.
土曜日＿＿ともだち＿＿でかけました。

Ask what time it is and then answer.

2.25 PM

Invite someone to go to the park with you.

Say 'Yesterday, today, tomorrow, last week, this week, next week.'

せんしゅうの　金曜日に としょかんで べんきょうしました。
What did you do? Where? When?

Say that you ate sushi at a Japanese restaurant.

Ask a friend to have lunch with you tomorrow.

＿＿＿に　テレビの ニュースを　みます。
Supply a time for the sentence.

Invite someone to come to your home next week.

Suggest to a friend that you go to town at 10.30.

Name four places you can go after school.

Say 'Last month, this month, next month, last year, this year, next year.'

ごご　四時五分前に こうえんで　あいましょう。
What is suggested to do? When? Where?

Invite a friend to sing a song together.

ゴール

スコア

14-18	9-13	0-8
すごいですね。 Congratulations! You are the champion!	もうちょっと… Nearly there! Go over the questions that you got wrong.	がんばって！ Go over the ぶんぽう & たんご page. Good luck!

01

十四

02

ひっこし！

In this unit, you will learn to:

ask and say where something or someone is

ask if something or someone is in a particular place and answer when someone asks you

ask and describe what something is like

describe what is in your room

write a letter in Japanese

recognise and write the kanji characters: 上, 下, 中, 前

In this unit, you will learn about:

grammatical differences of Japanese and English adjectives

Japanese housing

Japanese addresses

Yuki has moved from Tokyo to Yamaguchi. She sends a postcard and a letter to her friend, Daisuke, to tell him about her new home.

「みて！はがきです。ゆきさんから！」

ひっこしを　しました。
あたらしい　じゅうしょです。
あそびに　きてください。

〒753-0046
山口県　山口市　本町　1905番地
電話　　083-973-0472

だいすけくんへ、
こんにちは。おげんきですか。
わたしは　いま　あたらしい　うちに　すんでいます。とても
すてきです。わたしの　あたらしい　うちは　山口（やまぐち）に　あります。
しずかな　まちです。東京（とうきょう）の　アパートは　とても
ちいさかったです。でも、あたらしい　うちは　とても
ひろいです。いまも　だいどころも　おおきいです。ちいさい
たたみの　へやも　あります。きれいな　にわも　ありますよ。
にわの　しゃしんを　みてください。いもうとと　いぬが　います。
いぬの　なまえは　「ポチ」です。かわいい　いぬでしょう。

don't you think?

わたしの　へやは　とても　あかるいです。へやに　ベッドと
つくえと　いすと　本だなと　テレビと　DVD プレーヤーが
あります。ベッドの　上に　ぬいぐるみが　たくさん
あります。くまや　いぬや　パンダなどです。わたしは
ぬいぐるみが　だいすきです。つくえの　よこに
本だなが　あります。本だなの　中に　まんがや
ざっしや　DVD が　たくさん　あります。つくえの　上に
でんきスタンドや　コンピューターが　あります。

a lot
bear

わたしは　あたらしい　うちが　だいすきです。でも、まだ
ともだちが　いません。ちょっと　さびしいです。みんなに
また　あいたいです。だいすけくん、みんなと　いっしょに
あそびに　きませんか。

but/not yet

I want to see you again.

Won't you come and play?

じゃあ、またね
3月17日　金曜日
まつだ　ゆきより

〒194-0021
東京都　町田市　中町　5丁目　485-9
本田　だいすけ 様

While unpacking her belongings, Yuki misplaces several items.

02

十
七

しりませんよ .... I don't know

Comic by Mami Yamanaka

Questions

1 Where is Yuki's new home?
2 How does she compare her old home and her new one?
3 What is her new home like?
4 Describe Yuki's room.
5 What is on Yuki's bed?
6 What is on the bookshelf?
7 What does Yuki keep on her desk?
8 How is Yuki feeling?
9 When did Yuki write the letter?
10 What is Yuki looking for?

れんしゅう

01 Asking and saying something or someone is in a particular place

一 うちに　おかあさんが　いますか。
　　はい、います。

二 にわに　ねこが　いますか。
　　いいえ、いません。いぬが　います。

三 へやに　つくえが　ありますか。
　　はい、あります。

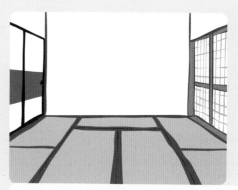

四 たたみの　へやに　とけいが
　　ありますか。
　　いいえ、ありません。

02 Asking or saying where something or someone is

一 いぬは　どこに　いますか。
　　いすの　よこに　います。

二 じしょは　どこに　ありますか。
　　つくえの　上に　あります。

03 Describing what is in your room

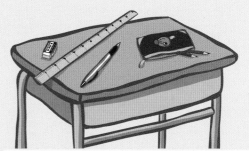

一 へやに 何が ありますか。
　ざっしや とけいや ごみばこなどが
　あります。

二 つくえの 上に 何が ありますか。
　ふでばこと ペンと けしごむと
　ものさしが あります。

04 Asking and saying what something or someone is like

一 どんな へやですか。
　あかるい へやです。

二 どんな いぬですか。
　かわいい いぬです。

三 どんな コンピューターですか。
　べんりな コンピューターです。

四 どんな ねこですか。
　しずかな ねこです。

02

十
九

漢字
かんじ

These are the kanji and their readings introduced in this unit.

A person standing above the line.

一	十	上					

上に → うえに → above/on top of
テーブルの　上に → テーブルの　うえに → on top of the table
はこの　上に → はこの　うえに → above the box
いすの　上に　あります。 → いすの　うえに　あります。 → It is on top of the chair.

A person hanging upside down below the line.

一	丁	下					

下に → したに → below/under
ベッドの　下に → ベッドの　したに → below the bed
テレビの　下に → テレビの　したに → under the TV
つくえの　下に　あります。 → つくえの　したに　あります。 → It is under the desk.

なか／チュウ　inside/in the middle

A person standing in the middle of a circle.

丨	口	口	中				

中に → なかに → in the middle of/inside
うちの　中に → うちの　なかに → inside the house
はこの　中に　あります。 → はこの　なかに　あります。 → It is inside the box.
じゅぎょう中 → じゅぎょうちゅう → during class

まえ／ゼン　in front of/before

Two people standing in front of a house.

丶	丷	斗	广	前	前	前
前						

前に → まえに → in front of/before
うちの　前に → うちの　まえに → in front of the house
な前 → なまえ → name

02

二
十

ぶんぽう

Asking if something or someone is in a particular place

へやに　しゃしんが　ありますか。
Are there photos in the room?

本だなの　上に　テレビが　ありますか。
Is there a TV on top of the bookshelf?

にわに　いぬが　いますか。
Is there a dog in the garden?

いすの　前に　ねこが　いますか。
Is there a cat in front of the chair?

Responding that something or someone is in a particular place

はい、あります。　(non-moving things)
Yes, there is.

いいえ、ありません。
No, there isn't.

はい、います。　(living things)
Yes, there is.

いいえ、いません。
No, there isn't.

Asking where something or someone is

コンピューターは　どこに　ありますか。
Where is the computer?

おとうさんは　どこに　いますか。
Where is Dad?

Saying where something or someone is

コンピューターは　つくえの　上に　あります。
The computer is on top of the desk.

おとうさんは　にわに　います。
Dad is in the garden.

Asking what is in a place

へやに　何が　ありますか。
What is in the room?

Saying what is in a place

へやに　しんぶんと　ざっしと　本が　あります。
There are newspapers, magazines and books in the room.

つくえの　上に　ふでばこや　でんきスタンドなどが　あります。
On the desk there is a pencil case and a lamp, among other things.

Asking what something is like

どんな　うちですか。
What kind of house is it?

Saying what something is like

ひろい　うちです。
It is a spacious house.

すてきな　うちです。
It is a wonderful house.

は and が

These have no English meaning. They are important grammar tools in Japanese. The easiest way to handle them in this unit is to remember this:

は テレビは　いまに　あります。
The TV is in the living room.

が いまに　テレビが　あります。
There is a TV in the living room.

Use が when the English uses 'there is' or 'there are'.

Use は when you mention the noun first.

House and Rooms

アパート	flat/unit/apartment
いま	living room
うち	house
しんしつ	bedroom
だいどころ	kitchen
たたみの　へや	tatami room
トイレ	toilet
にわ	garden
へや	room
マンション	apartment/apartment building
ようしつ	Western-style room
わしつ	Japanese-style room

Furniture and objects found in a room

いす	chair
えんぴつ	pencil
けいたいでんわ	mobile phone
けしごむ	eraser
ごみばこ	rubbish bin
コンピューター	computer
ざっし	magazine
ざぶとん	cushion
じしょ	dictionary
しゃしん	photo
しんぶん	newspaper
つくえ	desk
DVDプレーヤー	DVD player
テーブル	table
テレビ	TV
でんきスタンド	lamp
とこのま	Japanese alcove
とけい	clock
ぬいぐるみ	soft toy
はがき	postcard
はこ	box
ふでばこ	pencil case
ふとん	Japanese bed
ベッド	bed
本だな	bookshelf
本ばこ	bookcase
ものさし	ruler

Locations

上	above
いすの　上に	on top of the chair
下	below
ベッドの　下に	under the bed
中	inside
へやの　中に	in the room
前	in front of
本だなの　前に	in front of the bookshelf
うしろ	behind
つくえの　うしろに	behind the desk
そと	outside
うちの　そとに	outside the house
よこ	next to
テレビの　よこに	next to the TV
となり	next to (similar items)
にわの　となりに	next to the garden

Describing words

あかるい	bright
あたらしい	new
いい	good
うるさい	noisy
おおきい	big
かわいい	cute
きたない	dirty
きれい（な）	pretty/clean
くらい	dark
しずか（な）	quiet
すき（な）	likeable (favourite)
すてき（な）	wonderful
せまい	narrow
ちいさい	small
どんな	What kind of ...?
ひろい	spacious
ふるい	old
べんり（な）	convenient
わるい	bad

The past tense of いい is よかった.

文法
ぶんぽう Plus

あります and います

These two words mean the same so how are they different? Can you guess from these examples?

うち　　ぬいぐるみ
へや　**あります**　つくえ
　　ほん　　えんぴつ

　　　ともだち　おかあさん
ねこ　**います**
おにいさん　　いぬ

Have you guessed?

あります is used for inanimate objects – things that can't move around by themselves. This also includes trees and plants.

います is used for animals and people – even if they are not alive anymore!

Adjectives

DID YOU NOTICE some adjectives end in い and others use な? Confusing, yes – but VERY IMPORTANT to remember because the two types have different grammatical rules. How are they used?

• SOMETHING THE SAME → both are followed by です.

E.g.　おおきいです。　　　(It is big.)
　　　しずかです。　　　　(It is quiet.)

• SOMETHING DIFFERENT → one needs to use な before a noun.

E.g.　おおきい　うちです。　(It is a big house.)
　　　すてき**な**　うちです。　(It is a wonderful house.)

It isn't easy to remember which type is which but if an adjective ends in い then usually it doesn't use な. A few exceptions to this rule are きれい, きらい, ゆうめい, とくい etc.

Particle Panic

と and や both mean AND but the difference is:

• と means you have to name all the items
• や means you only have to name some of them.

For example:

テーブルの　上に　ペンと　えんぴつと　はさみと　けしごむと　ものさしと　ふでばこが　あります。
(On the table there are pens, pencils, scissors, an eraser, a ruler and a pencil case.)

テーブルの　上に　ペンや　けしごむや　ものさしなどが　あります。
(On the table there is a pen, eraser, ruler etc.)

02

二十三

23

てがみをかきましょう。

opening phrases for letters

Dear Ikuzo
いくぞうさん／くんへ、

How are you?
おげんきですか。

It's been a long time.
ひさしぶりですね。

I'm sorry I haven't written to you for a long time.
ながい　あいだ、てがみを　かかなくて　すみませんでした。

Thank you very much for your letter.
てがみを　どうも　ありがとう　ございました。

Last week/yesterday Yuki's letter came.
せんしゅう／きのう　ゆきさんから　てがみが　きました。

closing phrases

Please send me a letter.
てがみを　ください。

Please write back soon.
おへんじを　かいてください。

I'm looking forward to your reply.
おへんじを　たのしみに　しています。

Give my regards to your family.
ごかぞくに　どうぞ　よろしく。

Take care of yourself.
おからだに　きを　つけて。

See you later.
じゃあ、また。

Year	Month	Day
2007年	2月	10日
Month	Day	Day of the week
2月	10日	月曜日

From Kenji
けんじより

わたしのうち

PROFILE

traditional

1st floor (ground floor in Australia)
2nd Floor (1st floor in Australia)

わたしの　うちは　ひろしまに　あります。
とても　でんとうてきな　うちです。
ちちと　ははと　いもうとと　そぼと
いっしょに　すんでいます。とても　ひろい
うちです。うちの　前に　にわが
あります。一かいに　たたみの　へやと
だいどころと　いまと　トイレと　おふろと
そぼの　へやが　あります。二かいに
わたしの　へやと　ちちと　ははの　へやと
いもうとの　へやと　トイレが　あります。
わたしの　へやは　いもうとの　へやの
となりに　あります。わたしの　へやは
ようしつです。とても　あかるいです。
わたしの　うちが　だいすきです。

ぼくのうち

PROFILE

ぼくの　かぞくは　三人かぞくです。
ちちと　ははと　ぼくです。マンションに
すんでいます。
ぼくの　マンションは　ちょっと
ちいさいです。マンションの　前に
きっさてんや　みせが　あります。とても
べんりです。トイレと　おふろと
だいどころと　いまと　バルコニーと
わしつと　ようしつが　あります。
わしつは　ちちと　ははの　へやです。
ようしつは　ぼくの　へやです。
ぼくの　へやに　キーボードが　あります。
よく、ともだちと　うたを　うたいます。

02

二十五

25

Daisuke writes a letter to Yuki.

Daisuke's reply

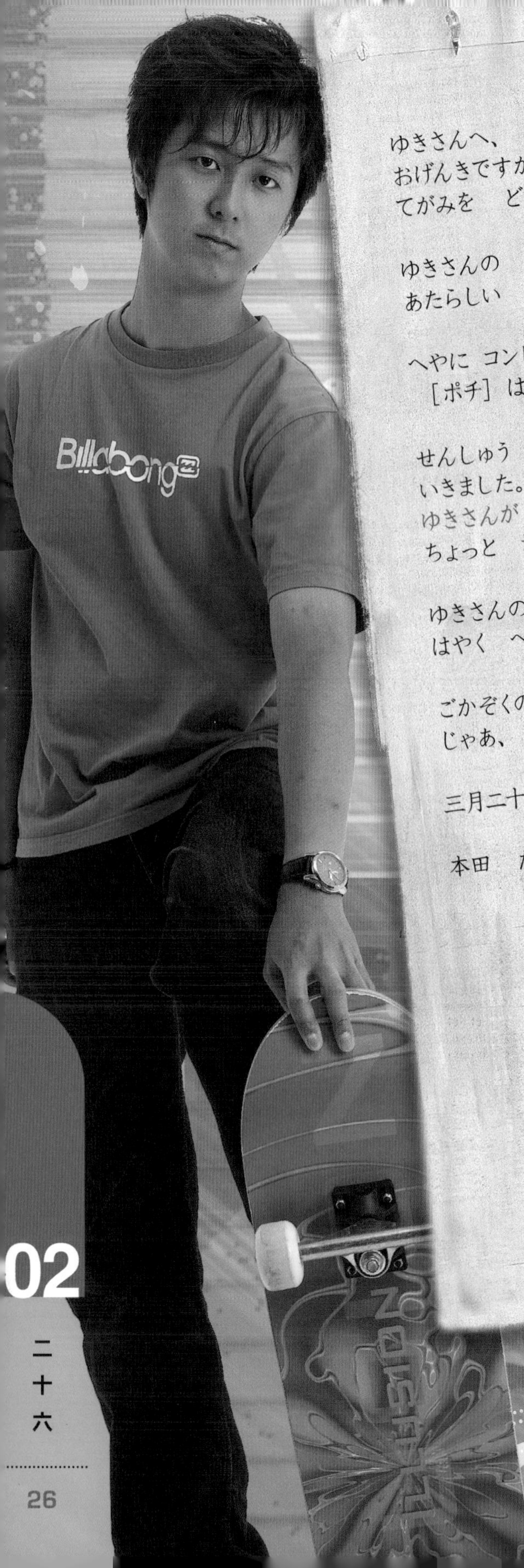

ゆきさんへ、
おげんきですか。 きのう ゆきさんの てがみが きました。
てがみを　どうも　ありがとう。

ゆきさんの　あたらしい　うちの　しゃしんを　みました。
あたらしい　うちは　いいですね。 ぼくの　うちは　せまいです。

へやに コンピューターが　ありますね。 いいなあ。
［ポチ］は かわいい　いぬですね！

せんしゅう　けんいちくんと　いっしょに　えいがに
いきました。 えいがは　とても よかったです。 でも、
ゆきさんが　いません。 だから、けんいちくんは
ちょっと　さびしいそうです。

ゆきさんの　あたらしい　Ｅメールアドレスは　何ですか。
はやく　へんじを　くださいね。

ごかぞくの　みなさんに　どうぞよろしく。
じゃあ、また。

三月二十一日　　火曜日

本田　だいすけより

movie

Yuki is not here

seems sad

02

03

あたらしい学校

In this unit, you will learn to:

ask about someone's year grade and respond when someone asks you

ask about school subjects and respond when someone asks you

use から and まで when talking about specific times

ask what something or someone is like and respond in the negative

express your opinion about the best and the most

ask the reason why and respond

recognise and write the kanji characters: 学 , 校 , 年 , 生

In this unit, you will learn about:

the similarities and differences of school life in Japan and Australia

the Japanese way of conducting an interview

Yuki went to an orientation day at her new school. She was interviewed by a teacher.

インタビュー

Teacher: ゆきさんは　何年生ですか。

Yuki: わたしは　中学（ちゅうがく）三年生です。

T: あ、三年生ですか。どんな　かもくを　べんきょうしていますか。

Y: えいごと　こくごと　れきしと　すうがくと　かがくと　おんがくと
びじゅつと　たいいくを　べんきょうしています。

T: そうですか。ちりは　べんきょうしていますか。

Y: いいえ、ちりは　べんきょうしていません。

T: そうですか。らいしゅうから　ちりを　べんきょうしますよ。

Y: ああ、そうですか。ちりは　むずかしいですか。

T: いいえ、むずかしくないです。たのしいですよ。

T: 一ばん　とくいな　かもくは　何ですか。

Y: ええと、一ばん　とくいな　かもくは　えいごです。

T: あら、そう？　なぜですか。

Y: えいごの　せんせいは　とても　おもしろいです。きびしくないです。
そして、えいごの　うたを　うたいます。ゲームも　します。だから、
えいごが　だいすきです。

T: そうですか。あたらしい　えいごの　せんせいも　とても
やさしいですよ。

Y: えー。よかった。

the study of your mother tongue

umm
Oh, really?
very
(We) also play games.

Really? Great!

03

二十八

T: 一ばん　にがてな　かもくは　何ですか。

Y: たいいくです。あんまり　とくいじゃないです。

T: そうですか。たいいくの　せんせいも　やさしいですよ。
じゃあ、しつもんが　ありますか。

Y: はい、あります。学校は　何時から　何時までですか。

T: 学校は　ごぜん　八時四十分から　ごご　三時三十五分までです。
これは　時かんわりです。どうぞ。

Y: ありがとうございます。

Do you have questions?

Here is your timetable.

南 中学校　じかんわり
（みなみちゅう）

		月曜日	火曜日	水曜日	木曜日	金曜日
ホームルーム	8:40-8:50					
一時かんめ	8:55-9:45	かがく	すうがく	ちり	えいご	こくご
二時かんめ	9:55-10:45	れきし	えいご	こくご	かがく	びじゅつ
三時かんめ	10:55-11:45	ちり	かがく	ほけん	すうがく	れきし
四時かんめ	11:55-12:45	こくご	おんがく	すうがく	かていか	えいご
ひる休み	12:45-1:20					
五時かんめ	1:25-2:15	すうがく	たいいく	かていか	こくご	すうがく
六時かんめ	2:25-3:15	えいごコミュニケーション	びじゅつ	かがく	すうがく	たいいく
ホームルーム／そうじ	3:15-3:35		びじゅつ	かがく	おんがく	たいいく

Questions

1. What year grade is Yuki? What subjects is she studying now?

2. What is Yuki's best subject? Why?

3. What is her weakest subject?

4. What question does Yuki ask the teacher?

5. How can you tell that this is not a conversation between friends?

6. What do you notice about the Japanese timetable?

7. In what way is it similar to yours and in what way is it different?

03

二十九

れんしゅう

01 Asking someone's year grade and responding

一　何年生ですか。
中学　三年生です。

二　ティーナさんは　何年生ですか。
しょうがく　六年生です。

三　だいすけくんは　何年生ですか。
こうこう　一年生です。

四　ゆりさんは　何年生ですか。
だいがく　一年生です。

02 Asking someone what subject s/he is studying and responding

えいご
すうがく
おんがく
かがく
たいいく
日本ご

一　どんな　かもくを　べんきょうしていますか。
えいごと　すうがくと　おんがくと　かがくと　たいいくと
日本ごを　べんきょうしています。

二　どんな　かもくを　べんきょうしていますか。
えいごや　すうがくや　日本ごなどを　べんきょうしています。

03 Asking and saying when something starts and finishes

一時かんめ　8:50から

ひる休み　1:40まで

学校　8:30～3:30

キャンプ　水曜日から金曜日まで

一　一時かんめは　何時からですか。
八時五十分からです。

二　ひる休みは　何時までですか。
ごご　一時四十分までです。

三　学校は　何時から　何時までですか。
八時半から　三時半までです。

四　キャンプは　いつから　いつまでですか。
水曜日から　金曜日までです。

03

れんしゅう

04 Asking what something or someone is like and responding in the negative

一　すうがくは　むずかしいですか。
　　いいえ、むずかしくないです。

二　たいいくの　せんせいは　きびしいですか。
　　いいえ、きびしくないです。やさしいです。

三　日本ごの　クラスは　しずかですか。
　　いいえ、あんまり　しずかじゃないです。

四　ゆきさんは　スポーツが　とくいですか。
　　いいえ、ぜんぜん　とくいじゃないです。

05 Comparing and saying the best/most ...

一　一ばん　すきな　かもくは　何ですか。
　　一ばん　すきな　かもくは　日本ごです。

二　一ばん　むずかしい　かもくは　何ですか。
　　一ばん　むずかしい　かもくは　れきしです。

三　一ばん　きびしい　せんせいは　だれですか。
　　一ばん　きびしい　せんせいは　えいごの　せんせいです。

四　一ばん　にがてな　かもくは　何ですか。
　　一ばん　にがてな　かもくは　すうがくです。

06 Asking the reason why and responding

一　なぜ　ちりが　すきですか。
　　ちりは　おもしろいです。だから、ちりが　すきです。

二　なぜ　日本ごが　すきですか。
　　ゲームを　します。だから、日本ごが　すきです。

三　なぜ　かていかは　たのしいですか。
　　おいしい　りょうりを　たべます。だから、
　　かていかは　たのしいです。

四　なぜ　きのう　おべんとうを　かいませんでしたか。
　　おべんとうは　すきじゃないです。だから、かいませんでした。

03

三十一

かんじ

These are the kanji and their readings introduced in this unit.

 学

A child reading a book under the roof with three rain drops.

`	`	``	``	``	``	学
学						

中学 → ちゅうがく → junior high school
すう学 → すうがく → maths
か学 → かがく → science

 校

Every school has trees and students.

一	十	才	木	木	朳	栌	栌
栌	校						

学校 → がっこう → school
こう校 → こうこう → senior high school

 年

Once a year, you can cut your birthday cake.

ノ	ゲ	ゲ	午	缶	年		

一年 → いちねん → one year
二年半 → にねんはん → two and a half years
何年 → なんねん → How many years?
こ年 → ことし → this year

 生

A student with a pen in his hand.

ノ	ゲ	牛	牛	生			

何年生 → なんねんせい → What year grade?
九年生 → きゅうねんせい → Year 9
七年生から → ななねんせいから → from Year 7
十年生まで → じゅうねんせいまで → to Year 10

03

三十二

文法

ぶんぽう

Asking someone's year grade

何年生ですか。
What year grade are you?

Saying what year grade you are

わたしは 中学 三年生です。
I am a Year 3 student at junior high school (Year 9).

Asking what subjects someone is studying

どんな かもくを べんきょうしていますか。
What subjects are you studying?

Saying what subjects you are studying

えいごと すうがくと れきしと おんがくを べんきょうしています。
I am studying English, maths, history and music.

Asking when something starts and finishes

学校は 何時から 何時までですか。
What time does school start and finish?

Saying when something starts and finishes

学校は ごぜん 八時半から ごご 三時二十五分までです。
School is from 8:30 am to 3:25 pm.

Describing something in the negative (い adjectives)

日本ごは むずかしくないです。
Japanese is not difficult.

Describing something in the negative (な adjectives)

おんがくの クラスは しずかじゃないです。
Music class in not quiet.

Saying what is the best/most ... (い adjectives)

一ばん おもしろい かもくは かがくです。
The most interesting subject is science.

Saying what is the best/most ... (な adjectives)

一ばん すきな かもくは びじゅつです。
My favourite subject is visual art.

Asking why

なぜ 日本ごが すきですか。
Why do you like Japanese?

Giving a reason

ゲームを します。だから、日本ごが すきです。
We play games. That's why I like Japanese.

03

三十三

えいご
English

日本ご
Japanese

フランスご
French

イタリアご
Italian

コンピューター
computer
(information technology)

すうがく
maths

かがく
science

かていか
home economics

おんがく
music

れきし
history

ちり
geography

けいざい
economics

びじゅつ
visual art

ぎじゅつ
design and technology

たいいく
physical education

ほけん
personal development

単語
たんご

Timetable terms

ホームルーム	Home room
一時かんめ	Period 1
二時かんめ	Period 2
三時かんめ	Period 3
四時かんめ	Period 4
ひる休み	Lunch break
五時かんめ	Period 5
六時かんめ	Period 6
そうじ	Clean up
クラブかつどう	Club activity
ほうかご	after school

い adjectives

	good		not good
いい	good	よくない	not good
うるさい	noisy	うるさくない	not noisy
おもしろい	interesting	おもしろくない	not interesting
きびしい	strict	きびしくない	not strict
たのしい	fun	たのしくない	not fun
つまらない	boring	つまらなくない	not boring
むずかしい	difficult	むずかしくない	not difficult
やさしい	kind/easy	やさしくない	not kind/easy
わるい	bad	わるくない	not bad

な adjectives

きらい（な）	dislike	きらいじゃない	don't dislike
きれい（な）	pretty/clean	きれいじゃない	not pretty/clean
しずか（な）	quiet	しずかじゃない	not quiet
すき（な）	like/favourite	すきじゃない	don't like
すてき（な）	nice	すてきじゃない	not nice
でんとうてき（な）	traditional	でんとうてきじゃない	not traditional
とくい（な）	good at	とくいじゃない	not good at
べんり（な）	convenient	べんりじゃない	not convenient
にがて（な）	bad at	にがてじゃない	not bad at
ゆうめい（な）	famous	ゆうめいじゃない	not famous

School

しょうがく	primary shool
中学	middle school/ junior high school
こうこう	high school

Year grades

Japanese year grades		English			Australian year grades
しょうがく	一年生 二年生 三年生 四年生 五年生 六年生	Primary School	Yr 1 Yr 2 Yr 3 Yr 4 Yr 5 Yr 6		一年生 二年生 三年生 四年生 五年生 六年生
ちゅうがく	一年生 二年生 三年生	Junior High School	Yr 1 Yr 2 Yr 3	Yr 7 Yr 8 Yr 9	七年生 八年生 九年生
こうこう	一年生 二年生 三年生	Senior High School	Yr 1 Yr 2 Yr 3	Yr 10 Yr 11 Yr 12	十年生 十一年生 十二年生
だいがく	一年生 二年生 三年生 四年生	University	Yr 1 Yr 2 Yr 3 Yr 4	Yr 1 Yr 2 Yr 3	一年生 二年生 三年生

03

三十五

文法

ぶんぽう Plus

There is a subtle difference between these pairs of words

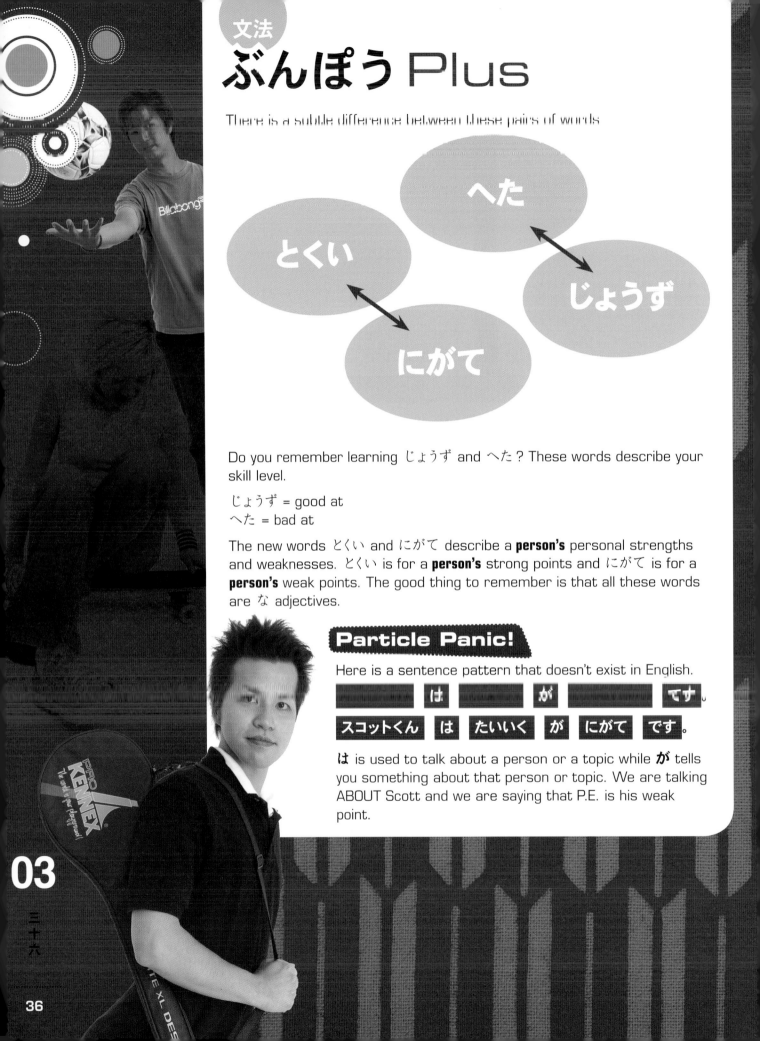

へた

とくい

じょうず

にがて

Do you remember learning じょうず and へた？ These words describe your skill level.

じょうず = good at
へた = bad at

The new words とくい and にがて describe a **person's** personal strengths and weaknesses. とくい is for a **person's** strong points and にがて is for a **person's** weak points. The good thing to remember is that all these words are な adjectives.

Particle Panic!

Here is a sentence pattern that doesn't exist in English.

| ▮ | は | ▮ | が | ▮ | です | 。 |

| スコットくん | は | たいいく | が | にがて | です | 。 |

は is used to talk about a person or a topic while **が** tells you something about that person or topic. We are talking ABOUT Scott and we are saying that P.E. is his weak point.

03

三十六

ぼくの学校プロフィール

こんにちは。ぼくは にしむら　たかしです。
ぼくは　こうりつこうこうの　一年生です。
まい日、九時から　二時まで　アルバイトを　しています。
きっさてんの　アルバイトです。だから　ぼくは
ていせいの　学校で　べんきょうしています。

ていせいの 学校は
ごご　五時半から 九時までです。
学校で すうがくや こくごや かがくや
ちりを べんきょうしています。学校の　あとで
しゅくだいを します。たいへんです。でも、
がんばります。

せんせいしょうかい

わたしの　せんせいを　しょうかいします。
トンプソンせんせいです。一ばん　おもしろい
えいごの　せんせいです。オーストラリアから
きました。二十六さいです。えいごの　クラスは
とても　たのしいです。ときどき　ゲームを　します。
だから、えいごの　クラスは　しずかじゃないです。トンプソンせんせいは
ちょっと　きびしいです。だから、　みんな　かならず　えいごの
しゅくだいを　します。

一ばん　すきな　ともだち

わたしの　一ばん　すきな　ともだちは　ひなちゃんです。ひなちゃんは
しょうがく　三年生からの　ともだちです。いま、ラサールこうこうで
べんきょうしています。こうこう　一年生です。
ラサールこうこうは　しりつの学校です。とても、でんとうてきな　学校です。
まい日　しゅくだいが　たくさん　あります。せんせいも　きびしいです。
ひなちゃんの　一ばん　とくいな　かもくは　すうがくです。
だから　ひなちゃんは　すうがくが　だいすきです。でも、
すうがくは　むずかしいです。だから、ときどき
ひなちゃんが　わたしの　しゅくだいを
します。いいですね。ひなちゃんが　だいすきです。

03

すごろくをしませんか。

スタート

Answer the question
何年生ですか。

What is 一時かんめ？

たかこさんは
こうこう　一年生です。
What year is Takako?

Name four subjects offered at your school.

Name four different い adjectives.

Say what subjects you study.

Say that Japanese is not difficult.

Name four different な adjectives.

Say that maths is not easy.

おひる休みは
十二時四十五分から
一時半までです。
How long is the lunch break?

わたしの　学校は
あまり　ゆうめいじゃない
です。What is the school like?

Write the kanji for 'year'.

Answer the question.
学校は　何時から
何時までですか。

Say that you like ice-cream and that's why you bought it.

Say the reason why you like that subject.

Say what subject you like the best?

Write the kanji for 'school'.

ゴール

スコア		
13-17	8-12	0-7
すごいですね。Congratulations! You are the champion!	もうちょっと…Nearly there! Go over the questions that you got wrong.	がんばって！Go over the ぶんぽう & たんご page. Good luck!

04

きせつ

In this unit, you will learn to:

ask and say which season or object you prefer

ask and say what you are going to do

ask and say what the weather is like

ask and say what the weather was like

ask about and predict what the weather will be like in the future

ask about temperature and respond

ask and say what someone would like or not like to do

recognise and write the kanji characters: 春 , 夏 , 秋 , 冬

In this unit, you will learn about:

Japanese onomatopoeia

Japanese haiku poetry and Japanese proverbs relating to the weather

seasonal traditions in Japan

きせつ

春 はなみツアー

九州の　春の　てんきは
いいですよ。
さくらを　みに　きませんか。
4日かんの　りょこう：
一人　¥80 000 から

まい日　いろいろな　こうえんに
いきます。きれいな　さくらの　はなを
みましょう。ともだちと　いっしょに
ピクニックを　しませんか。
カラオケパーティーも　あります。

さくら...................	cherry blossoms
4日かん......................	four days

冬 わくわくおんせん

さむい　冬が
きました。
あたたかい　おんせんは
どうですか。きもちが　いい
ろてんぶろに　はいりませんか。
からだに　いいですよ。
3日かんの　りょこう
一人　¥60 000 から

しょくじつき
ばんごはんは　わしょく
あさごはんは　ようしょく
まい日　リラックスしましょう。

わくわく..............................	exciting
きもちが　いい	
ろてんぶろ...........	a relaxing outdoor bath
からだに　いいですよ....	good for your body
3日かん.............................	three days
しょくじつき....................	meals included
わしょく.........................	Japanese food
ようしょく.....................	Western food

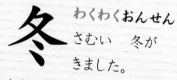

04

四十

秋 北海道キャンプ

じょうばや　やまのぼりや　ハイキングなどが　できます。
北海道の　秋は　すばらしいです。

こくりつこうえんで　いろいろな　ことを　しましょう。やまに　こうようを
みに　いきませんか。おんせんも　あります。どうぞ　北海道に　きてくださいね。

スケジュール
一日め：ひこうきで　東京から　さっぽろへ
二日め：ごぜん　じょうば　ごご　ピクニック、
　　　　こうようの　しゃしんを　とりましょう
三日め：こくりつこうえんハイキング／やまのぼり
四日め：ごぜん　じゆうこうどう　ごご　東京に　かえります
一人　¥60 000

こくりつこうえん .... national park

いろいろな　こと .... various things

こうよう .... the changing colour of autumn leaves

一日め .... the first day

じゆうこうどう .... free time

南中学校の ニュース
つばさくんの　夏休みレポート

七月二十一日から　二十七日まで
月曜日：十時まで　ねました。あつかったからです。ごご、けんいちくんと　うみに　およぎに　いきました。
水曜日：けんたくんと　かわに　つりに　いきました。たのしかったです。ぼくと　けんたくんは　つりが　だいすきです。
　　　　でも　さかなが　つれませんでした。ざんねんでした。
日曜日：ちえこさんの　かぞくと　たまがわで　はなびを　みました。かきごおりを　たべました。

七月二十八日から　八月三日まで
火曜日：ちえこさんの　おとうさんの　ボートで　水上スキーを　しました。とても　よかったです。
木曜日：ぼくの　たんじょうびでした。ちちと　ははから　あたらしい　じてんしゃを　もらいました。
　　　　ごご、みんなで　こうえんに　あそびに　いきました。サイクリングを　しました。
土曜日：ちちの　ともだちの　うちで　バーベキューを　しました。おいしかったです。ステーキと　サラダを　たべました。
　　　　ジュースと　コーラを　のみました。にわで　いぬと　あそびました。それから、あとで　ちちの　くるまで
　　　　ドライブに　いきました。

あつかったから .... because it was hot

つれませんでした。 ......I couldn't catch any

ざんねんでした。 .... It was disappointing

かきごおり ....shaved ice treat

水上スキー .... waterskiing

もらいました .... received

あとで .... after

Questions

1　Look at the travel brochures. How much does each tour cost and what activities are available?

2　What is the schedule for the camping tour of Hokkaido?

3　What kind of holiday did Tsubasa's family finally take?

4　Describe four activities he did during this holiday?

04

四十一

練習
れんしゅう

01 Asking and saying which one

一 どの　きせつが　すきですか。
春が　すきです。

二 この　しゃしんを　とりましたか。
はい、とりました。

三 その　くるまは　だれのですか。
あにの　くるまです。

四 あの　さかなを　たべましたか。
はい、たべました。

02 Asking and saying what you are going to do

一 夏休みに　ハイキングに　いきますか。
はい、やまに　ハイキングに　いきます。

二 しゅうまつに　うみに　およぎに　いきますか。
はい、いきます。

三 あした　何を　しますか。
まちに　あそびに　いきます。いっしょに
いきませんか。

03 Asking and saying what the weather is or is not like

一 きょうの　てんきは　どうですか。
いい　てんきですよ。きょうは　はれです。
さむくないです。

二 こんやの　てんきは　どうですか。
いやな　てんきですよ。くもり　ときどき　あめです。

04 Asking and saying what the weather was or was not like

一 きのうの　てんきは　どうでしたか。
きのうは　くもり　のち　あめでした。
むしあつかったです。

二 せんしゅうは　いい　てんきでしたか。
いいえ、いやな　てんきでしたよ。
かぜが　つよかったです。

04

四十二

れんしゅう 🔘

05 Asking and predicting what the weather will be like in the future

一 あしたの　てんきよほうです。
　　広島は　はれでしょう。
二 大阪は　あめ　のち　くもりでしょう。
三 北海道の　てんきは　どうでしょうか。
　　北海道は　くもり　ときどき　ゆきでしょう。
四 あしたは　ゆきでしょう。
　　ごごは　かぜが　つよいでしょう。

06 Asking and talking about the temperature

一 きのうの　きおんは　何どでしたか。
　　三十二どでした。あつかったですね。
二 きょうの　さいてい　きおんは　何どですか。
　　れいどです。とても、さむいですね。
三 あしたの　さいこう　きおんは　何どでしょうか。
　　十六どでしょう。すこし　すずしいでしょう。

07 Asking and saying what someone would like to do

一 あめです。何を　したいですか。
　　DVDを　みたいです。
二 夏休みに　何を　したいですか。
　　りょこうを　したいです。
三 いい　てんきですね。テニスを　しましょう。
　　テニスですか。あんまり　したくないです。

04

四十三

春

Three people in the sun.

一	二	三	夫	夫	表	春	春
春							

春休み → はるやすみ → spring holiday
春子 → はるこ → Haruko
春まき → はるまき → spring roll
春が すきです。 → はるが すきです。 → I like spring.

 夏

Think of setting up your umbrella and towel and seat in the summer sun. Go nuts on the beach in summer.

一	一	一	一	百	百	百	百
夏	夏						

夏休み → なつやすみ → summer holiday
夏の いろ → なつの いろ → summer colours
夏子 → なつこ → Natsuko
夏は あついです。 → なつは あついです。 → Summer is hot.

 秋

Imagine roasting chestnuts by a tree.

一	二	千	千	禾	禾	秒	秋
秋							

秋休み → あきやずみ → autumn holiday
秋まつり → あきまつり → autumn festival
秋子 → あきこ → Akiko
秋は きれいです。 → あきは きれいです。 → Autumn is pretty.

 冬

Two people skiing on the slopes in winter. Who is skiing? You!

ノ	ク	久	冬	冬			

冬休み → ふゆやすみ → winter holiday
冬の たべもの → ふゆの たべもの → winter food
冬が すきです。 → ふゆが すきです。 → I like winter.
冬は さむいです。 → ふゆは さむいです。 → Winter is cold.

文法
ぶんぽう

Asking and saying which one

どの DVD を みましたか。
Which DVD did you watch?

Responding

この DVD を みました。
I watched this DVD.

その DVD を みました。
I watched that DVD.

あの DVD を みました。
I watched that DVD over there.

Saying what you are going to do

ともだちの うちに あそびに いきます。
I will go to my friend's house to play.

Asking what the weather is or is not like

きょうの てんきは どうですか。
What is today's weather like?

Responding

いい てんきですよ。きょうは はれです。
さむくないです。
It's good weather. Today is sunny. It isn't cold.

いやな てんきですよ。くもり ときどき あめです。
It's awful weather. It's cloudy and sometimes rainy.

Asking what the weather will be like in the future

あしたの てんきは どうでしょうか。
What will tomorrow's weather be like?

Predicting what the weather will be like in the future

はれ のち くもりでしょう。
It will probably be sunny and cloudy later.

! These expressions are used in weather reports.

Asking what the weather was or was not like

きのうの てんきは どうでしたか。
What was yesterday's weather like?

せんしゅうは いい てんきでしたか。
Was it good weather last week?

Responding

きのうは はれ のち くもりでした。
むしあつかったです。
Yesterday was sunny and later cloudy.
It was hot and humid.

いいえ、いやな てんきでした。
No, it was awful weather.

Asking the temperature

さいてい きおんは 何どですか。
What is the lowest/minimum temperature?

さいこう きおんは 何どですか。
What is the highest/maximum temperature?

Talking about the temperature

さいてい きおんは れいどです。
The lowest temperature is zero degrees.

さいこう きおんは 三十五どです
The highest temperature is 35 degrees.

Asking what someone would like to do

きょうは あめですね。何を したいですか。
It's raining today. What do you want to do?

Responding

水えいを したいです。
I want to swim.

りょうりを したくないです。
I don't want to cook.

04

四十五

45

単語
たんご

Seasons

きせつ	seasons
春	spring
夏	summer
秋	autumn
冬	winter

Adjectives

あたたかい	warm
あつい	hot
いい	good
いそがしい	busy
いや (な)	awful
さむい	cold
すごい	amazing
すずしい	cool
すばらしい	wonderful
むしあつい	hot and humid
わるい	bad

Weather

あめ	rainy
あめ　ときどき　ゆき	rain and occasional snow
あらし	stormy
かぜが　つよい	strong wind
くもり	cloudy
たいふう	typhoon
はれ	sunny
はれのちくもり	sunny and cloudy later
ふぶき	blizzard
ゆき	snowy

Temperature

さいこうきおん	the highest temperature
さいていきおん	the lowest temperature
何ど	What temperature?
～ど	degrees (celcius)
れいど	zero degrees

04

Activities you might do during the different seasons.

春

こうえんに はなみに いきます。	I will go to the park to go flower viewing.
おんせんに はいります。	I will get into a hot spring.
サイクリングを します。	I will go cycling.
こくりつこうえんで じょうばを します。	I will go horse riding in a national park.
りょこうを します。	I will travel.
にわで ねます。	I will sleep in the garden.
りょうりを します。	I will cook.
さんぽを します。	I will go for a walk.
ハイキングを します。	I will go hiking.
やまのぼりを します。	I will go mountain climbing.

夏

うみに サーフィンに いきます。	I will go to the beach to surf.
はなびを みに いきます。	I will go to see the fireworks.
かわに つりに いきます。	I will go to the river to fish.
ボートに のります。	I will ride in a boat.
水上スキーを します。	I will waterski.
うみで およぎます。	I will swim at the beach.
水えいを します。	I will have a swim.
リラックスします。	I will relax.
ともだちと あそびます。	I will play with my friend.
ともだちと でかけます。	I will go out with my friends.
エアコンを つけます。	I will switch on the airconditioner.
せんぷうきを けします。	I will switch off the fan.
かさを かいます。	I will buy an umbrella.

秋

やまに ドライブに いきます。	I will go to the mountains for a drive.
秋まつりで やきいもを たべます。	I will eat roast sweet potato at an autumn festival.
やまのぼりを します。	I will go mountain climbing.
しゅうがくりょこうに いきます。	I will go on a school excursion.
こうようは すばらしいです。だから やまに いきます。	The autumn colours are wonderful. So, we'll go to the mountains to see them.
よるは さむくないです。 だから にわで おつきみを しましょう。	The evening is not cold so let's look at the moon in the garden.

冬

おもちを たべます。	I will eat rice cakes.
おかしを たべます。	I will eat sweets.
スキーを します。	I will ski.
スノーボードを します。	I will snowboard.
ゆきだるまを つくります。	I will make a snowman.
トランプを します。	I will play cards.
ピアノを ひきます。	I will play the piano.
としょかんに いきます。	I will go to the library.
ヒーターを つけます。	I will switch on the heater.

文法
ぶんぽう Plus

Watch out for these words!

どれ、これ、それ、あれ

As you saw in the ぶんぽう section of this unit, どの means 'which'. It is used in sentences like 「どの　DVD が　すきですか」 (Which DVD do you like?). You might reply 「この　DVD が　すきです」 (I like this DVD).

The important thing to remember about どの is that you need to connect it to a noun. In the above example どの is connected to 'DVD'. どれ, on the other hand, also means 'which' but it does not need to be connected to a noun. For example, 「どれが　すきですか」 (Which do you like?). You might reply 「これが　すきです」 (I like this).

The following examples might help you remember the difference between these two patterns:

どの　えが　すきですか。	Which picture do you like?
この　えが　すきです。	I like **this** picture.
その　えが　すきです。	I like **that** picture.
あの　えが　すきです。	I like **that** picture **over there**.

どれが　すきですか。	Which do you like?
これが　すきです。	I like **this**.
それが　すきです。	I like **that**.
あれが　すきです。	I like **that over there**.

The many faces of に

You have learnt to use particle **に** in two ways.

For example,
- for a specific time: 六時に　たべます。
- going to a place: やまに　いきます。

HOWEVER, に can also be used when you are going to a place to do an activity.

For example:
- Place に activity に　いきます。

Study the examples below:

やまに　ドライブに　いきます。(I am going to the mountains for a drive.)

うみに　およぎに　いきます。(I am going to the beach to swim.)

! The activity can be a noun or a verb stem like あそび from あそびます or およぎ from およぎます.

ぶんぽう Plus

です／でしょう

When you say IT IS, you use です.

For example:

きょうは　あめです。(It is rainy today.)

However, when you say IT SHOULD BE or IT PROBABLY WILL, then use でしょう. でしょう means PROBABLY and is used to indicate uncertainty.

For example:

あしたは　あめでしょう。(It will probably rain tomorrow.)

I want to/I don't want to

When you want to say I WANT TO or I DON'T WANT TO do something, these examples will show you how.

いき	ます	I will go
	たいです	I WANT to go
	たくないです	I DON'T WANT to go

Choose the ending you want.

Tenses make you tense

	い adjectives		な adjectives	
is	あつい	is hot	いや	is awful
isn't	あつくない	isn't hot	いやじゃない	isn't awful
was	あつかった	was hot	いやでした	was awful
wasn't	あつくなかった	wasn't hot	いやじゃなかった	wasn't awful

Analyse the similarities and differences between the endings used by each type of describing word. Both use ない and なかった and the past endings all have た. Once you see the pattern, look for a clue to help you remember the differences.

04

四十九

49

はいく

Originating in the fourteenth century, haiku poetry conveys a rich image using very few words. It is often used to write about the seasons and has evolved to become a three-line poetic form made of 5, 7, 5 syllables. Here are some examples in English and Japanese.

Beautiful sunshine
I lie on a picnic rug
Feeling so happy

The park is changing
Autumn turns red
and yellow
A carpet of leaves

秋の　たべもの
おいしいよ
あつい　うどんを
たべましょう

秋の　いろ
あか、きいろ
もみじの　はっぱ
うつくしい

秋まつり
秋まつり
よいやさ、よいさ
にぎやかね

春かぜで
さくらの　はなが
ちりました

夏の　うみ
あかい　ボートに
のりました

あつい　夏
アイスクリームを
たべたいよ

ともだちと
キャンプに　いきます
にぎやかね

ゆきだるま
かわいそうね
さむいから

04

Onomatopoeia

Here are some onomatopoeia relating to the weather.

1 ぽかぽか

2 ぎらぎら

3 たらたら

4 ぽつぽつ

5 しとしと

6 ざあざあ

7 びゅーびゅー

8 さむざむ

9 ぶるぶる

10 こんこん

11 カチンコチン

1 warmth
2 pulsating heat from the sun
3 sweating
4 light drops of rain
5 sprinkling rain
6 heavy rain
7 strong wind
8 chilly, draughty
9 shivering
10 heavy snow
11 freezing up

04

五十一

51

冬

おせちりょうり New Year food

おいしい！　おしょう月の　たべものです。
たべませんか。

Special New Year food is eaten cold. This allows everyone to relax on New Year's day. The food is beautifully presented on a four-tiered lacquer box.

かどまつ／しめかざり New Year decorations

みなさん、あけまして　おめでとう。

This New Year decoration is made from bamboo, pine and straw.

It is displayed on each side of the front gate or door. The pine is a symbol of long life. The twisted rope is hung over the door of the house to bring good luck.

こたつ Japanese heater

こたつが　あります。
だから　さむくないです。

This heater has an infrared light under the table which heats the air. The air is trapped by the quilt. Everyone sits at the table and puts their hands and feet under the quilt to keep warm. The heater is very efficient and cheap to run. In summer the table is used as normal.

New Year Cards

Japanese often send Christmas cards these days but the really important tradition is the sending of New Year cards. Look at these examples.

あけまして
おめでとうございます！

ことしも　よろしく
おねがいします。

ちえこさんへ
あけまして　おめでとう　ございます！
いま　さっぽろは　とても　さむいです。
らいしゅう　かぞくと　スキーに　いきます。
ちえこさんも　きませんか。
でんわしてね。
ことしも　よろしくね。
ゆき　より

お年玉

春

ひなにんぎょう Girl's Day dolls

学校の　あとで　パーティーを　しましょう。

These dolls are displayed on Girl's Day 〔三月三日〕 and represent the Emperor and Empress. They are displayed to pray for the happiness and good health of the girls in the family.

おはなみ Flower viewing

はなみを　しましょう。
いっしょに　ピクニックを
しませんか。カラオケで
うたを　うたいました。
はずかしかったです。

This is a time for picnics in the open air to celebrate the coming of spring.

五月にんぎょう Boy's Day decorations

五月五日は　休みでした。
たのしかったですよ。

These dolls include samurai armour or helmets and other items needed to fight battles in olden items. They are displayed to pray for the bravery and courage of the boys in the family.

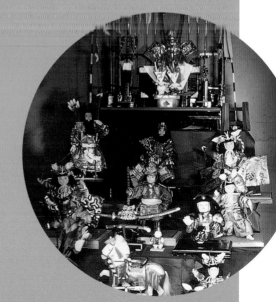

夏

はなび Fireworks

どうして　夏が　一ばん　すきな
きせつですか。
たのしいですから。はなびが
たのしみです。

Fireworks are a traditional part of summer festivals.

たなばた Star festival

おもしろい　はなしですよ。おりがみの　ほしを
つくりましょう。

This is the one day of the year when the Weaver Princess star crosses the path of the Cowherd star. These stars were lovers and were separated by the River of Heaven (the Milky Way) and on this night they renew their love for each other.

しょちゅうみまい
Mid-season greetings

休みは　ながいですよ。はがきを
かきましょう。

うちわ Fans

ゆかたを　きて、
よみせに　いきます。

These are often available at festivals and are designed with many colourful traditional patterns and logos.

秋

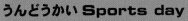

ぶんかさい
Cultural day

学校に　あそびに
いきましょう。

Schools all over Japan celebrate learning by arranging displays, games and food stalls for visitors who come to the school on this Open Day.

うんどうかい Sports day

秋は　うんどうかいの　きせつです。
あつくないですからね！

On this day, schools and communities are involved in lots of different games.

秋まつり
Autumn harvest festival

一ばん　にぎやかな
おまつりは　秋まつりです。

This is a celebration of a good harvest which means a time of prosperity for everyone. It is the traditional way to give thanks.

おつきみ Moon viewing

どうして　おつきみが　すきですか。
おつきみの　パーティーは　たのしいですから。

When the moon is full in autumn many families like to admire it in the cool of the evening. Decoration of rice dumplings, pampas grass and autumn fruit are displayed.

04

日本の　しぜん

Natural phenomena of Japan

春一ばん

春一ばん are strong winds which blow during spring. The word was originally used by Japanese fishermen because of the rough seas caused by the wind. It is now a commonly used term to describe weather.

かみなり

かみなり (lightning) often brings rain and sudden drops in temperature. かみなり is an old favourite in Japanese folk tales. The concept of かみなり originated because of the many storms in summer when people did not wear heavy clothes. It was considered dangerous to walk around or to sleep without covering one's tummy because it was believed that かみなり liked to take people's belly buttons!

つゆ

In early summer, cold wind from the north-east and warm air from the south-west come together over Japan bringing heavy rain. This rainy season is called つゆ and normally lasts about a month. Although this season is considered a nuisance by some people, it is essential for farmers' crops.

つなみ

Tidal waves are produced by earthquakes occurring under the ocean. The word つなみ is now used internationally. The biggest つなみ in Japan was the めいじさんりくつなみ recorded in 1896. The waves were more than 20 metres high and were reported to have claimed 26 360 victims. つなみ travel faster in deeper water. For example at depths of 1 000m, the speed is 1.5 times that of the しんかんせん which is more than 200km/hour.

じしん

Earthquakes are one of the most feared natural disasters in Japan. Japan is situated on the intersection of three tectonic plates and is therefore prone to earthquakes. Over 1 000 earthquakes per year occur in Japan.

Two of Japan's most notable Earthquakes are the Great Kanto Earthquake in 1923 and more recently, the Kobe Earthquake in 1995. The Kobe Earthquake was described as one of the costliest natural disasters in history.

Along with fire drills, earthquake drills are regularly practised in schools and companies. Students are instructed to think quickly, switch off the electricity and gas, open all doors and take shelter under furniture until the earthquake stops.

たいふう

Tropical depressions sometimes develop into tropical storms. A large-scale storm in Asia is called たいふう (typhoon). In the USA, Canada, Europe and Great Britain, there are ハリケーン (hurricanes) and in Australia there are サイクロン (cyclones). サイクロン and たいふう can be seen from satellites.

かざん

There are a number of active volcanoes throughout Japan. ふげんだけ in the north of Kyushu erupted in 1990 after being dormant for over 200 years. In June 1991, it erupted again. 39 people were killed and three people were declared missing, including some famous vulcanologists who were studying the mountain. Houses were burned under the lava and the area was severely damaged. Mt Fuji is a dormant かざん. It last erupted in 1707.

05

たんじょうびのプレゼント

In this unit, you will learn to:

ask and say what someone can do

ask how much an item costs and answer when someone asks you

count, understand, read and write numbers to 10 000 000

recognise different types of verbs and use them in a new pattern

order and purchase items in a shop

recognise and write the kanji characters: 百 , 千 , 万 , 円

In this unit, you will learn about:

counting large numbers

Japanese currency

shopping

Yuko rings Megumi to get her help. Together they go shopping to buy a present for Yoko's brother Kenji.

かいものに　いきますか。

もしもし

はい、もしもし。
あ、ようこさん
ですか。

はい、そうです。
あのね、あした
いそがしいですか。

ええと、なぜですか。

あの、日曜日は、おとうとの
たんじょうびです。だから
プレゼントを　かいたいです。
いっしょに　まちに
かいものに　いきませんか。

Umm ...

ああ、いいですね。
でも、ごぜん　九時から
ごご　二時ごろまで
じゅくに　いきます。
だから、三時ごろから
いけますよ。

ほんとうですか。
じゃ、いっしょに
....
いきましょう。

about

cram school

ねえ、ようこさん、
おとうとさんは
何年生ですか。

けんじは
中学　二年生です。
けんじは　スポーツが
すきです。

へえ、そうですか。
じゃ、サーフィンの
みせに　いきましょう。
もうすぐ　夏です。

soon

05

C-ric by Kenny Chan

swimwear

expensive

cheap

デパートで

too expensive

It is a pity.

Oh, I remember
something!

五十七

05

Questions

1 What time do Megumi and Yoko arrange to go shopping?

2 When is Kenji's birthday?

3 Does Yoko buy bathers for Kenji?

4 What does Megumi suggest instead?

5 Where do they buy it?

6 How much does the present cost?

05

れんしゅう

01　Asking how much an item costs and responding

¥200

¥1 200

¥185 000

$3.50

一　これは　いくらですか。
　　はい、これは　二百円です。

二　この CD は　いくらですか。
　　千二百円です。

三　この　コンピューターは　いくらですか。
　　十八万五千円です。

四　アイスクリームは　いくらですか。
　　三ドル五十セントです。

02　Asking and saying what you can do

8.00am

一　日本ごが　よめますか。
　　はい、よめます。

二　すしが　食べられますか。
　　はい、たべられます。

三　水えいが　できますか。
　　はい、すこし　できます。

四　ごぜん　八時に　こられますか。
　　いいえ、いけません。

漢字
かんじ

These are the kanji and their readings introduced in this unit.

ヒャク／ビャク／ピャク 　100

One hundred jelly beans in a jar

三百	→	さんびゃく	→	300
六百	→	ろっぴゃく	→	600
八百	→	はっぴゃく	→	800

何百ですか。 → 　なんびゃくですか。 → 　How many hundreds?

セン／ゼン 　1000

A man sending 1000 signals.

三千	→	さんぜん	→	3 000
六千	→	ろくせん	→	6 000
八千	→	はっせん	→	8 000

何千ですか。 → 　なんぜんですか。 → 　How many thousands?

マン 　10 000

A man rollerblading.

一万	→	いちまん	→	10 000
五万	→	ごまん	→	50 000
百万	→	ひゃくまん	→	1 000 000

何万ですか。 → 　なんまんですか。 → 　How many ten thousands?

エン 　yen〔¥〕

Put some yen into your empty pocket.

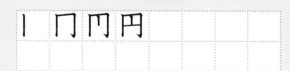

九十円	→	きゅうじゅうえん	→	¥90
二百十円	→	にひゃくじゅうえん	→	¥210
千二百円	→	せんにひゃくえん	→	¥1 200
百万円	→	ひゃくまんえん	→	¥1 000 000

文法
ぶんぽう

Asking how much an item costs

この　本は　いくらですか。
How much is this book?

その　DVDは　いくらですか。
How much is that DVD?

あの　ざっしは　いくらですか。
How much is that magazine?

Responding

その　本は　四百円です。
That book is 400 yen.

この　DVDは　五十円です。
This DVD is 50 yen.

あの　ざっしは　十二ドルです。
That magazine is 12 dollars.

Asking if someone can do something

ピアノが　ひけますか。
Can you play the piano?

日本ごの　しんぶんが　よめますか。
Can you read the Japanese newspaper?

二時の　でんしゃに　のれますか。
Can you catch the 2 o'clock train?

さかなが　たべられますか。
Can you eat fish?

このドアが　あけられますか。
Can you open this door?

この　えいがが　みられますか。
Can you watch this movie?

ゴルフが　できますか。
Can you play golf?

パーティーに　こられますか。
Can you come to the party?

Responding

はい、　ひけます。
Yes, I can (play the piano).

はい、　よめます。
Yes, I can (read it).

はい、　のれます。
Yes, I can (catch it).

はい、　たべられます。
Yes, I can (eat it).

はい、　あけられます。
Yes, I can (open it).

いいえ、　みられません。
No, I can't (watch it).

はい、　できます。
Yes, I can (play it).

はい、　いけます。
Yes, I can (go).

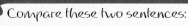

! Compare these two sentences:
さかなを　たべます。
さかなが　たべられます。
Not only does the verb form change but the particle does too – from を to が.

05

六十一

61

単語

たんご

Group 1 verbs

ます form	English	Can do	English
いいます	say/call	いえます	can say
かえります	return	かえれます	can return
ききます	listen	きけます	can listen
きります	cut	きれます	can cut
すわります	sit	すわれます	can sit
たちます	stand up	たてます	can stand up
つかいます	use	つかえます	can use
はいります	enter	はいれます	can enter
はなします	speak/talk	はなせます	can speak/talk
まちます	wait	まてます	can wait
もちます	carry/hold	もてます	can carry/hold

Group 2 verbs

ます form	English	Can do	English
あけます	open	あけられます	can open
おぼえます	remember	おぼえられます	can remember
かぞえます	count	かぞえられます	can count
しめます	close	しめられます	can close
つけます	turn on	つけられます	can turn on
つづけます	continue	つづけられます	can continue
みせます	show	みせられます	can show
みます	see	*みられます／みえます	*can see
でかけます	go out	でかけられます	can go out

Group 3 (irregular) verbs

ます form	English	Can do	English
うんてんします	drive	うんてんできます	can drive
きます	come	こられます	can come
そうじします	clean	そうじできます	can clean
でんわします	telephone	でんわできます	can telephone
リラックスします	relax	リラックスできます	can relax

! します *always becomes* できます。

! Why are the verbs divided up into different groups? Look at ぶんぽう Plus for more details.

! There is more than one way to say 'I can see' and 'I can hear' in Japanese – and they have quite different uses. Look at ぶんぽう Plus for an explanation.

05

六十二

文法
ぶんぽう Plus

What can you hear?

There are two ways of saying 'I can see' and 'I can hear' introduced in this unit. きけます (can listen) and みられます (can see) are used when you hear or see something with some effort – you have to consciously listen or look. However, きこえます (is audible) and みえます (is visible) are commonly used when you hear or see something without making any effort at all. Look at the examples:

こんばん　この　えいがが　みられます。(I can watch this movie tonight.)
You will make a conscious decision and effort to see the movie.

うちから　やまが　みえます。(I can see the mountains from the house.)
They are visible whether you specifically look for them or not.

What's a verb?

Verbs are action words – 'hear', 'eat', 'go' etc. All verbs in Japanese have an *i* sound or an *e* sound straight before the ます. Check this rule by looking at the romaji for each of the verbs below. Make a list of all the verbs you know and check this rule with them too. The rule will help you distinguish verbs from other words, and the rule applies regardless of which group a verb belongs to.

いきます (iki-masu)　　たべます (tabe-masu)　　かいます (kai-masu)
みます (mi-masu)　　のります (nori-masu)　　します (shi-masu)

Verb Groups

Verbs in Japanese can be divided into three groups, each with special characteristics. You need to know which group a verb belongs to when using it in different ways. In this unit, we use the basic ます form and adapt it to say 'I can do ...' It is handy to know how the verb groups work because the rules for adapting each verb to a new pattern depend entirely on which group it belongs to – and the rules vary for each group! Otherwise we would have to learn each verb one by one. The verb groups are: Group 1 verbs, Group 2 verbs and Group 3 (irregular) verbs. Some verbs are listed in their groups on the たんご page of this unit. The complete list of all the verbs introduced in Obento Supreme is on pages 166 and 167.

05

六十三

ぶんぽう Plus

Saying you can do an action – the potential form

As you have just seen, verbs can be divided into different groups. Each group has its own rules. Take care to use the correct rule for each verb when using the potential form.

Group 1 verbs		
Most of the verbs you know belong to this group. They all have an *i* sound before ます. To say 'I can …' change the *i* sound to an *e* sound.	かいます buy	かえます can buy
	はなします speak	はなせます can speak

Group 2 verbs		
These verbs generally have an *e* sound followed by ます. However, there are exceptions to this rule – there are a few Group 2 verbs that end in *i* - ます (if there is only one syllable before ます, it's probably Group 2). To say 'I can …' add られ between the *e* or *i* sound and ます.	たべます eat	たべられます can eat
	おきます wake up	おきられます can wake up

Group 3 (irregular) verbs		
These verbs have their own special rules for using this pattern. Fortunately, there are only two of them to remember!	します do/play	できます can do/play
	きます come	こられます can come

きます vs. きます

きます (to come) is a Group 3 verb, but きます (to wear) belongs to Group 2. How confusing! You need to hear or read them in context to figure out which word it is. However, once you have learnt the kanji for each one, it is obvious which is meant – 来ます (to come) or 着ます (to wear).

Large numbers

Although large numbers are rarely written completely in kanji today, they are always read as if they are!

たけしくんの　でんわばんごうは
何ですか？

9783-2105
きゅう なな はち さん の に いち ゼロ ご
九　七　八　三　・　二　一　０　五

トイレ
おふろ
キッチン
バルコニー

8万円
はち まん えん
八　万　円

96.5万円
きゅう じゅう ろく まん ご せん えん
九 十 六 万 五 千 円

¥725
なな ひゃく に じゅう ご えん
七百 二十 五 円

東京人口：12 000 000人
いっ せん に ひゃく まん にん
一 千 二 百 万 人

Special 100万円
ひゃく まん えん
百 万 円

いつ　オーストラリアに　いきましたか。
1999年に　いきました。
せん きゅうひゃくきゅうじゅう きゅう ねん
千 九百 九十 九 年

05

六
十
五

「あなたの まちから」

Anchor: じゃ、京都の さとうアナウンサーと はなしましょう。さとうさん、いま どこに いますか。

Reporter: こんにちは、なかやまさん。わたしは いま 京都の ゆうめいな 清水寺の ちかくに います。清水寺は この さかの 上に あります。この さかの なまえは 三年坂です。この さかの 下から 上まで あるいて 二十分ぐらい かかります。
三年坂には いろいろな みせが あります。おみやげや、おちゃわんが かえます。ちょっと みてみましょう。
すみません、これは かわいいですね。いくらですか。

Shopkeeper: はい、それは 八百五十円です。

Reporter: そうですか。じゃ、これは いくらですか。

Shopkeeper: それは 三千九百五十円です。

Reporter: そうですか。ありがとうございます。

Anchor: さとうさん、じゃ、清水寺の ほうへ いってください。

Reporter: はい、わかりました。
清水寺です。あそこに いりぐちが ありますね。あそこから はいれます。

Anchor: さとうさん、清水寺から 何が みえますか。

Reporter: はい、ここからの けしきを ちょっと みてみましょう。
すてきな けしきが みえますよ。あ、京都えきと 京都タワーが みえます。

Anchor: あれ、さとうさん、うしろから 何か きこえますね。何が きこえますか。

Reporter: はい、なかやまさん、これは かねの おとです。かねの おとが きこえます。あれ、ちょっと えいごが きこえますね。あ、がいこくからの かんこうきゃくです。清水寺は がいこくからの かんこうきゃくにも にんきが あります。

Anchor: へえ、そうですか。あの、さとうアナウンサー、時かんです。
京都からの レポートを どうも ありがとうございました。

announcer

Kiyomizu Temple/
near/slope
Sannen Hill

takes

souvenirs

tea cups/Let me
just check.

towards

over there/
entrance

here/scenery

Kyoto Station

Kyoto Tower

Umm .../
something

sounds of the big
gong

foreign tourist

popular

It's time.

report

05

六十六

06

どんな 人？

In this unit, you will learn to:

ask about and describe someone's physical appearance

ask about and describe someone's personality

ask what someone is wearing and answer

join い adjectives in extended descriptions

join な adjectives in extended descriptions

contrast characteristics

use colours in conversation and writing

write a personal letter

recognise and write the kanji characters: 手, 目, 耳, 口

In this unit, you will learn about:

differences in describing people between languages

colours across cultures and languages

Kayo is looking at pictures of Maki's host brother. Maki is trying to write a letter to him.

かよと　まきの　かいわ

Maki: ねえ、きいてください。わたしは　らい月から　オーストラリア人を　ホストします。

Kayo: へえ、その　人は　どんな　人ですか。

M: これは　わたしの　ホストブラザーの　しゃしんです。ロジャーくんです。これは　ロジャーくんの　かぞくと　ともだちの　しゃしんです。

K: へえ、みせてください。どれが　ロジャーくんですか。

M: この　人です。あかい　シャツを　きています。ロジャーくんは　せが　たかくて　かみが　ちゃいろです。

K: へえ、そうですか。ロジャーくんは　目が　おおきくて　やさしそうですね。かっこいいですね。

M: そうですね。ええと、ロジャーくんは　日本ごが　すこし　はなせます。スキーも　できます。だから、冬休みが　たのしみです。

K: いいですね。この　人は　ロジャーくんと　にていますね。はいいろの　Tシャツを　きて　ジーンズを　はいています。せが　たかくて　かみが　ちゃいろですね。だれですか。

M: ええと、この　人は　ロジャーくんの　おにいさんです。なまえは　ケンくんです。この　人は　ロジャーくんの　おとうさんです。おとうさんも　せが　たかいですね。これは　おかあさんです。ピンクの　ワンピースを　きています。おかあさんは　金ぱつですね。

to host

host brother

which?

looks kind/cool

to look forward to

to look alike

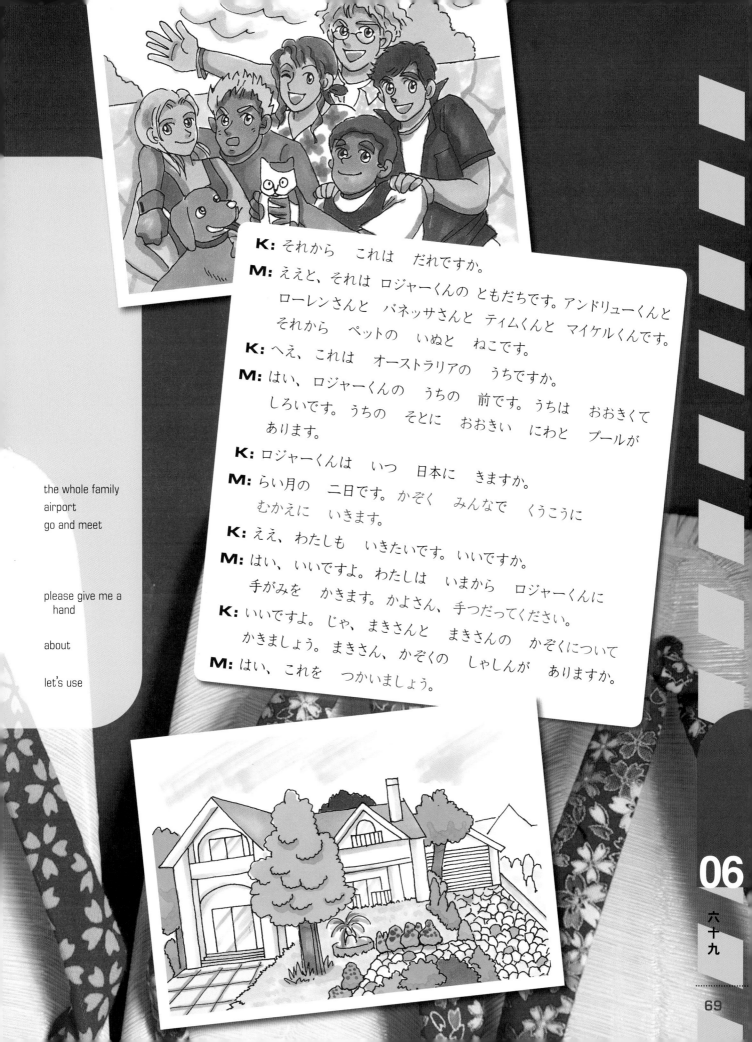

K: それから これは だれですか。

M: ええと、それは ロジャーくんの ともだちです。アンドリューくんと ローレンさんと バネッサさんと ティムくんと マイケルくんです。それから ペットの いぬと ねこです。

K: へえ、これは オーストラリアの うちですか。

M: はい、ロジャーくんの うちの 前です。うちは おおきくて しろいです。うちの そとに おおきい にわと プールが あります。

K: ロジャーくんは いつ 日本に きますか。

M: らい月の 二日です。かぞく みんなで くうこうに むかえに いきます。

K: ええ、わたしも いきたいです。いいですか。

M: はい、いいですよ。わたしは いまから ロジャーくんに 手がみを かきます。かよさん、手つだってください。

K: いいですよ。じゃ、まきさんと まきさんの かぞくについて かきましょう。まきさん、かぞくの しゃしんが ありますか。

M: はい、これを つかいましょう。

the whole family
airport
go and meet

please give me a
    hand

about

let's use

ロジャーくんへ、
おげんきですか。手がみを　ありがとう。わたしは　この手がみで
わたしと　わたしの　かぞくについて　かきます。

わたしの　かぞくは　四人です。ちちと　ははと　おとうとと
わたしです。ちちは　ちょっと　ふとっていますが、スポーツが
すきです。まい日　ごぜん　七時半から　ごご　八時ごろまで
しごとに　いきます。

ははは　かいものが　すきです。ははは　やせていて　せが
あまり　たかくないです。いつも　耳に　すてきな
イヤリングを　しています。りょうりが　上手で　いつも
いそがしいです。

おとうとは　十二さいです。しょうがく　六年生です。サッカーと
コンピューターゲームが　すきです。口が　おおきくて　いつも
うるさいです。

わたしは　まきです。十五さいです。中学　三年生です。
しゅみは　まんがと　バレーボールです。よく　ともだちと
でんわで　はなします。

ロジャー　くんに　あえるのを　たのしみに　しています。

らい月の　一日に　かぞく　みんなで　くうこうに　むかえに
いきます。

じゃ、さようなら。
十一月九日木曜日

まきより

fat

work

skinny

telephone

I'm looking forward
to seeing you.
to pick up

Questions

1　Who is in the photos Kayo and Maki are looking at?
2　What is Roger wearing?
3　What do Roger and Ken have in common?
4　How many people are there in Maki's family and who are they?

れんしゅう

01 Asking about someone's physical appearance and responding

一　たかこさんは　かみが　ながいですか。
　　はい、たかこさんは　かみが　ながいです。

二　ハジョーノくんは　せが　たかいですか。
　　いいえ、ハジョーノくんは　せが　あまり
　　たかくないです。

02 Asking the colour of someone's eyes and hair and responding

一　ケイトさんは　目が　くろいですか。
　　いいえ、ケイトさんは　目が　ちゃいろです。

二　ベンくんは　かみが　何いろですか。
　　ベンくんは　金ぱつです。

れんしゅう

03 Asking about someone's appearance and responding by linking adjectives

一　たかこさんは　どんな　人ですか。
　　たかこさんは　かみが　ながくて
　　めが　ちゃいろです。

二　すうがくの　せんせいは　どんな　せんせいですか。
　　すうがくの　せんせいは　しずかで　まじめです。

04 Describing someone with contrasting characteristics

一　おねえさんは　どんな　人ですか。
　　せが　たかくて　おもしろいですが、うるさいです。

06 Asking what someone is wearing and responding

一　きょうこさんは　何を　きていますか。
　　きょうこさんは　セーターと　コートを　きています。

二　かずきくんは　めがねを　かけていますか。
　　いいえ、かずきくんは　めがねを　かけていません。

かんじ

These are the kanji and their readings introduced in this unit.

 て **hand**

 手

A skeletal hand with a pen.

手紙	→	てがみ	→	letter
下手	→	へた	→	not skilled
上手	→	じょうず	→	skilled
みぎ手	→	みぎて	→	right hand

 め **eye**

 目

An eyeball in an eye socket.

ひだり目　→　ひだりめ　→　left eye
目を　あけてください。→　めを　あけてください。→　Please open your eyes.
目の　前　→　めの　まえ　→　in front of you
目が　おおきい。→　めが　おおきい。→　His/her eyes are big.

 みみ **ear**

 耳

An ear.

耳が　ちいさい。→　みみが　ちいさい。→　His/her ears are small.
耳が　とおい　→　みみが　とおい　→　hearing trouble

 ... ... くち **mouth**

口

A mouth.

口の　中　→　くちの　なか　→　inside the mouth
口が　おおきい。→　くちが　おおきい。→　His/her mouth is big.
口を　あけてください。→　くちを　あけてください。→　Please open your mouth.

06

七十三

ぶんぽう

Asking about someone's physical appearance

ひとみさんは　せが　たかいですか。
Is Hitomi tall?

ゆきさんは　かみが　くろいですか。
Does Yuki have black hair?

ゆうじくんは　かみが　ながいですか。
Is Yuji's hair long?

ベンくんは　目が　ちゃいろですか。
Are Ben's eyes brown?

Responding

はい、ひとみさんは　せが　たかいです。
Yes, Hitomi is tall.

はい、ゆきさんは　かみが　くろいです。
Yes, Yuki has black hair.

いいえ、ゆうじくんは　かみが　ながくないです。
No, Yuji's hair is not long.

いいえ、ベンくんは　目が　ちゃいろじゃないです。
No, Ben's eyes are not brown.

Asking the colour of someone's eyes and hair

ケイトさんは　目が　何いろですか。
What colour are Kate's eyes?

たかこさんは　かみが　何いろですか。
What colour is Takako's hair?

Responding

ケイトさんは　目が　あおいです。
Kate has blue eyes.

たかこさんは　かみが　くろいです。
Takako has black hair.

Describing people using two or more adjectives

ゆうこさんは　どんな　人ですか。
What kind of person is Yuko?

あなたの　せんせいは　どんな　人ですか。
What kind of person is your teacher?

サンタクロースは　どんな　人ですか。
What kind of person is Santa Claus?

いもうとさんは　どんな　人ですか。
What kind of person is your younger sister?

Responding

ゆうこさんは　せが　たかくて　かみが　ながいです。
Yuko is tall and she has long hair.

わたしの　せんせいは　かみが　みじかくて　からだが　おおきいです。
My teacher has short hair and he is big.

サンタクロースは　からだが　おおきくて　ひげが　ながいです。
Santa Claus is big and has a long beard.

いもうとは　目が　ちゃいろで　せが　ひくいです。
My younger sister has brown eyes and is short.

You need to be careful which adjectives you try to link! Look at ぶんぽう Plus for hints.

06

七十四

74

ぶんぽう

Describing someone with contrasting characteristics

シュレックは　こわいですが、　やさしいです。
Shrek is scary, but gentle.

わたしの　いぬは　小さくて　かわいいですが、
うるさいです。
My dog is small and cute, but noisy.

Asking what someone is wearing

ニコル・キッドマンは　何を　きていますか。
What is Nicole Kidman wearing?

Responding

ニコル・キッドマンは　きれいな　ドレスを
きています。
Nicole Kidman is wearing a pretty dress.

Asking if someone is wearing certain items

ようこさんは　コートを　きていますか。
Is Yoko wearing a coat?

きょうこさんは　ズボンを　はいていますか。
Is Kyoko wearing trousers?

きのう、ひろしくんは　スーツを　きていましたか。
Was Hiroshi wearing a suit yesterday?

パーティーで　リサさんは　あかい　くつを
はいていましたか。
Was Lisa wearing a red pair of shoes at the party?

Responding

はい、　ようこさんは　コートを　きています。
Yes, Yoko is wearing a coat.

いいえ、　きょうこさんは　ズボンを
はいていません。
No, Kyoko is not wearing trousers.

はい、　きのう　ひろしくんは　スーツを
きていました。
Yes, Hiroshi was wearing a suit yesterday.

いいえ、　パーティーで　リサさんは　くろい
くつを　はいていました。
No, Lisa was wearing black shoes at the party.

06

七十五

単語
たんご

からだ

あし	legs/feet
あたま	head
うで	arms
おしり	bottom
おなか	stomach
かた	shoulders
かみ（のけ）	hair
からだ	body
くび	neck
せなか	back
手	hands
ひざ	knees
ひじ	elbows
ゆび	fingers

かお

口	mouth
はな	nose
ひげ	beard
耳	ears
目	eyes

からだについて

かっこいい	attractive/trendy
せが　たかい	tall
せが　ひくい	short
ながい	long
ハンサム（な）	handsome
ふとっている	fat
ほそい	skinny/thin
みじかい	short
やせている	skinny/thin

せいかくについて

きびしい	strict
こわい	scary
たのしい	enjoyable/fun
のんき（な）	easy-going
へん（な）	strange
まじめ（な）	serious
やさしい	kind

Clothes

Tシャツ	T-shirt
セーター	sweater, woollen jumper
シャツ	shirt
ジャケット	jacket
ワンピース	(day) dress
みずぎ	bathers
くつ	shoes
ぞうり	thongs
ジーンズ	jeans
スカート	skirt
スニーカー	sneakers/runners
ズボン	trousers
パジャマ	pyjamas
ブーツ	boots

Accessories

アクセサリー	jewellery
イヤリング	earrings
ネクタイ	tie
時けい	watch
めがね	glasses
サングラス	sunglasses
ぼうし	hats

いろ – Colours

あか〔い〕	red
あお〔い〕	blue
きいろ〔い〕	yellow
くろ〔い〕	black
しろ〔い〕	white
みどり〔の〕	green
ちゃいろ〔の〕	brown
はいいろ〔の〕	grey
むらさき〔の〕	purple
ピンク〔の〕	pink
オレンジ〔の〕	orange
金ぱつ〔の〕	blond (hair)
ももいろ〔の〕	peach-coloured

! Colours aren't always what they seem! To find out more, look at the ぶんぽう Plus page.

Verbs

To put on	Wear/is wearing	Use with
きます	きています	Tシャツ／ドレス
はきます	はいています	ズボン／くつ
つけます	つけています	アクセサリー
かけます	かけています	めがね
かぶります	かぶっています	ぼうし
します	しています	ネクタイ／とけい

06

七十六

76

文法
ぶんぽう Plus

Using colours in a sentence

Some colours are い adjectives, so they use い adjective rules when used in sentences.

しんじくんは　目が　くろいです。(Shinji has black eyes.)
きいろい　Tシャツです。(It's a yellow T-shirt.)

Other colours are sometimes followed by の. These colours need の when they are followed by a noun.

ももいろの　ジャケットが　すきですか。(Do you like the pink jacket?)
はいいろの　くるまです。(It's a grey car.)

Talking about colours

In this unit, we have been describing things with colours, but what if you want to talk about the colour itself? English makes no differentiation between colours as adjectives (describing things) and colours as nouns (the name of the colour), but Japanese does. See if you can work out the different uses and the rules from these examples:

Colours used as adjectives:

あかい　くつが　すきです。(I like red shoes.)
みどりの　コートが　きらいです。(I don't like the green coat.)

Colours used as nouns:

あかが　すきです。(I like red.)
みどりが　きらいです。(I don't like green.)

> **!** Here's something to think about: are the names for colours used in exactly the same way in every language? Try investigating what Japanese people mean by あおい or ももいろ – are they used for the same colour range that English speakers think of as blues and pinks? Use a colour wheel to demonstrate what you find out. If they are not the same, why do you think they are translated as blue and pink?

Linking adjectives

What are the simple rules for joining adjectives to say things like 'fun and interesting', or 'quiet and pretty'?

い adjectives

Replace the い at the end with くて.

たのしい → たのしくて

な adjectives

Replace the な at the end with で.

しずかな → しずかで

Examples:

せんせいは　やさしくて　のんきです。(The teacher is kind and easy-going.)

しずかで　かわいい　いぬです。(It's a quiet, cute dog.)

> **!** When you join adjectives in this way, both adjectives must have the same (positive, negative or neutral) nuance. The second adjective can either be an い or a な adjective, regardless of the first one.

どんな人<ruby>人<rt>ひと</rt></ruby>？

07

いただきます

In this unit, you will learn to:

ask what someone is doing at the moment and respond

ask and say how many general items you want

ask and say how many items (in glasses or cups) you want

recognise and use common expressions at restaurants

recognise and write the kanji characters: 食 , 飲 , 行 , 買 , 大 , 小 , 安 , 高

In this unit, you will learn about:

the て form of verbs

more counters for common items

Japanese table manners

Japanese food

Japanese seasonal sweets

a Japanese recipe

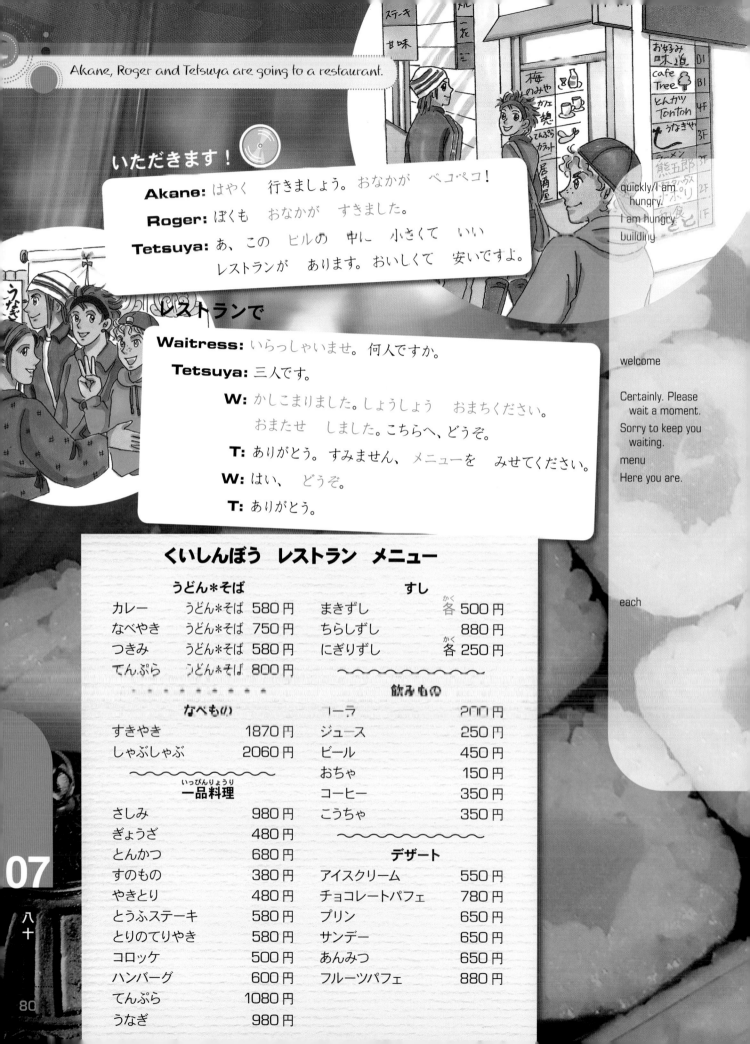

Akane, Roger and Tetsuya are going to a restaurant.

いただきます！

Akane: はやく　行きましょう。おなかが　ペコペコ！

Roger: ぼくも　おなかが　すきました。

Tetsuya: あ、この　ビルの　中に　小さくて　いい　レストランが　あります。おいしくて　安いですよ。

レストランで

Waitress: いらっしゃいませ。何人ですか。

Tetsuya: 三人です。

W: かしこまりました。しょうしょう　おまちください。おまたせ　しました。こちらへ、どうぞ。

T: ありがとう。すみません、メニューを　みせてください。

W: はい、どうぞ。

T: ありがとう。

quickly/I am hungry.
I am hungry.
building

welcome

Certainly. Please wait a moment.
Sorry to keep you waiting.
menu
Here you are.

each

くいしんぼう　レストラン　メニュー

うどん＊そば			すし		
カレー	うどん＊そば	580円	まきずし	各	500円
なべやき	うどん＊そば	750円	ちらしずし		880円
つきみ	うどん＊そば	580円	にぎりずし	各	250円
てんぷら	うどん＊そば	800円			

なべもの		飲みもの	
すきやき	1870円	コーラ	200円
しゃぶしゃぶ	2060円	ジュース	250円
		ビール	450円
一品料理（いっぴんりょうり）		おちゃ	150円
さしみ	980円	コーヒー	350円
ぎょうざ	480円	こうちゃ	350円
とんかつ	680円		
すのもの	380円	デザート	
やきとり	480円	アイスクリーム	550円
とうふステーキ	580円	チョコレートパフェ	780円
とりのてりやき	580円	プリン	650円
コロッケ	500円	サンデー	650円
ハンバーグ	600円	あんみつ	650円
てんぷら	1080円	フルーツパフェ	880円
うなぎ	980円		

udon noodles with curry sauce	**Akane:** ロジャーくんは　何に　しますか。
	Roger: ええと、ぼくは　カレーうどんに　します。あかねさんは　何に　しますか。
chicken skewers	**A:** わたしは　やきとりに　します。
one	**Tetsuya:** すみません、やきとりを　一つと　カレーうどんを　一つと　すしを　一つ　ください。飲みものは　ええと、
drinks	コーラを　ください。
How many glasses?	**Waitress:** 何ばいですか。
3 glasses	**R:** ええと、三ばいです。
	W: かしこまりました。
Cheers!	**All:** かんぱい！　いただきます！
Let's eat.	**T:** ロジャーくん、なまの　さかなが　食べられますか。
raw	**R:** はい、食べられますよ。
	A: あれ、ロジャーくん　何を　していますか。
	R: ええと、おはしを　つかっています。むずかしいですね。
chopsticks	**T:** ねえ、ロジャーくん、きょう　何を　しましたか。
	R: 買いものを　しました。本やで　じしょを　買いました。
bookshop	安くて　いい　じしょが　ありましたよ。
I've finished eating.	**All:** ごちそうさま。
I'm full.	**T:** おなかが　いっぱいです。
	A: すみません、いくらですか。
	W: はい、三千七百八十円です。ありがとうございます。
	A: ロジャーくん、何を　していますか。
	R: ええと、お金（かね）を　かぞえています。

07

八十一

Questions

1 Where was the restaurant they went to?
2 What did Roger order?
3 What kind of drinks and how many did they order?
4 Is Roger good at using chopsticks?
5 How much was the total bill?

れんしゅう 🔊

01 Asking what someone is doing and responding

一　何を　しています か。
　　本を　よんでいます。

二　何を　しています か。
　　テレビを　みています。

三　何を　しています か。
　　かんじを　れんしゅうしています。

02 Asking and saying how many general items you want

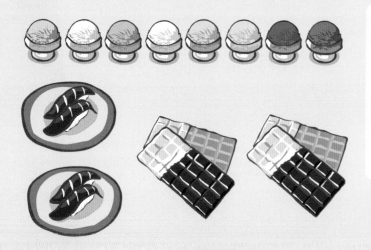

一　アイスクリームを　ください。
　　いくつですか。
　　八つです。

二　サーモンを　二つ　ください。
　　はい、かしこまりました。

三　チョコレートを　ください。
　　いくつですか。
　　四つ　おねがいします。

03 Asking and saying how many items (in glasses or cups) you want

一　おちゃを　ください。
　　何ばいですか。
　　二はいです。

二　すみません。水を　ください。
　　何ばいですか。
　　一ぱいです。

三　すみません。コーヒー　おねがいします。
　　いくつですか。
　　三つ　おねがいします。

れんしゅう 🔘

04 Asking for a specific quantity of an item in a shop or a restaurant

一　ハンバーガーを　二つ　ください。
　　ハンバーガーを　二つですね。かしこまりました。

二　コーラを　四はい　ください。
　　コーラを　四はいですね。はい、かしこまりした。

三　おにぎりを　三つと　ジュースを　二つ　ください。
　　おにぎりを　三つと　ジュースを　二つですね。
　　かしこまりました。

05 Asking and saying what you decided on

一　いらっしゃいませ。何に　しますか。
　　すしと　てんぷらを　ください。

二　いらっしゃいませ。何に　しますか。
　　ピザ　一つと　コーラを　二はい　ください。
　　はい、かしこまりした。

三　飲みものは　何に　しますか。
　　レモネードを　二はい　おねがいします。

かんじ

These are the kanji and their readings introduced in this unit.

た（べます）　to eat

Tho roof of a rootaurant with a cake.

ノ	𠆢	𠆢	今	今	今	食	食
食							

カンガルーは　くさを　食べます。→　カンガルーは　くさを　たべます。→　Kangaroos eat grass.
食べたいです。　→　たべたいです。→　I want to eat.
食べもの　→　たべもの　→　food
ケーキを　食べましょう。→　ケーキを　たべましょう。→　Let's eat a cake.

の（みます）　to drink

A waiter in a restaurant serves the drinks.

ノ	𠆢	𠆢	今	今	今	食	食
飠	飲	飲	飲				

おちゃが　飲みたいです。→　おちゃが　のみたいです。→　I want to drink tea.
飲みもの　→　のみもの　→　drinks
コーラを　飲みませんか。→　コーラを　のみませんか。→　Won't you drink cola?
飲んでください。→　のんでください。→　Please drink.

い（きます）　to go

行　行

An intersection with three roads.

ノ	ク	イ	彳	行	行		

パーティーに　行きたいです。　→　パーティーに　いきたいです。→　I want to go to a party.
いっしょに　行きましょう。→　いっしょに　いきましょう。→　Let's go together.
バスで　行きます。　→　バスで　いきます。　→　I will go by bus.

か（います）　to buy

A man carrying many boxes after shopping – three boxes on top and three underneath.

丨	冂	罒	罒	罒	罒	買	買
買	買	買	買				

買いもの　→　かいもの　→　shopping
買いたいです。→　かいたいです。→　I want to buy (it).
買いました。→　かいました。→　I bought (it).
買ってください　→　かってください。→　Please buy (it).

漢字
かんじ

These are the kanji and their readings introduced in this unit.

おお（きい）／ダイ big

The fish I caught was this big.

一	ナ	大		

大あめ	→	おおあめ	→	heavy rain
大ゆき	→	おおゆき	→	heavy snow
大人	→	おとな	→	adult
大学	→	だいがく	→	university

ちい（さい）／ショウ small

The fish I caught was this small.

亅	小	小		

小さい　いす	→	ちいさい　いす	→	small chair
手が　小さい。	→	てが　ちいさい。	→	S/he has small hands.
小学校	→	しょうがっこう	→	primary school

やす（い） cheap

A woman calling people to a bargain shop.

丶	宀	宀	灾	安	安

安い　ホテル	→	やすい　ホテル	→	cheap hotel
これは　安いです。	→	これは　やすいです。	→	This is cheap.
安いですか。	→	やすいですか。	→	Is it cheap?
安かったです。	→	やすかったです。	→	It was cheap.

たか（い）／コウ high/tall/expensive

A tall building is expensive.

丶	亠	亠	亣	古	产	高	高
高	高						

高い　レストラン	→	たかい　レストラン	→	expensive restaurant
それは　高いです。	→	それは　たかいです。	→	That is expensive.
高かったですか。	→	たかかったですか。	→	Was it expensive?
高校	→	こうこう	→	senior high school

07

八十五

85

Asking what someone is doing

ロジャーくんは　何を　していますか。
What are you doing/playing, Roger?

ともだちは　何を　みていますか。
What is your friend watching?

Responding

本を　よんでいます。
I am reading a book.

ともだちは　テレビを　みています。
My friend is watching TV.

Asking and saying how many items (in glasses or in cups) you want

何ばいですか。
How many glasses do you want?

Responding

一ぱいです。
One.

Asking for a specific quantity of an item in a shop or a restaurant

サーモンを　三つと　おちゃを　二はい　ください。
Three serves of salmon and two cups of tea please.

Asking and saying what you've decided on

何に　しますか。
What will you have?

すしと　おちゃに　します。
I'll have sushi and tea.

Asking and saying how many (general) items you want

いくつですか。
How many do you want?

Responding

一つです。
One.

> ! いくつ is used to ask how many general items you want. 何ばい is used to ask how many items you want in glasses or cups.

Counting general items

一つ (ひと)	1
二つ (ふた)	2
三つ (みっ)	3
四つ (よっ)	4
五つ (いつ)	5
六つ (むっ)	6
七つ (なな)	7
八つ (やっ)	8
九つ (ここの)	9
十 (とお)	10
十一 (じゅういち)	11
十二 (じゅうに)	12

Counting glasses or cups of drink

一ぱい (いっ)	1 glass/cup
二はい (に)	2 glasses/cups
三ばい (さん)	3 glasses/cups
四はい (よん)	4 glasses/cups
五はい (ご)	5 glasses/cups
六ぱい (ろっ)	6 glasses/cups
七はい (なな)	7 glasses/cups
八ぱい (はっ)	8 glasses/cups
九はい (きゅう)	9 glasses/cups
十ぱい (じゅっ)	10 glasses/cups
十一ぱい (じゅういっ)	11 glasses/cups

> ! Did you notice the way items are counted up to 10? This way of counting uses kun yomi, Japanese pronunciations, dating from before the Chinese influence on the Japanese language. They all end in a つ sound, except for 10! After 10, the counters are pronounced in the familiar way: 11 (じゅう いち), 12 (じゅうに) etc.

07

単語
たんご

The て form

Group 1 verbs

ます form	English	て form
あいます	meet	あって
あそびます	play	あそんで
いいます	say/call	いって
行きます	go	行って
うたいます	sing	うたって
およぎます	swim	およいで
買います	buy	買って
かえります	return	かえって
かきます	write	かいて
ききます	listen	きいて
きります	cut	きって
けします	turn off	けして
さわります	touch	さわって
すわります	sit	すわって
たちます	stand up	たって
つかいます	use	つかって
つくります	make	つくって
とります	take	とって
飲みます	drink	飲んで
のります	ride	のって
はいります	enter	はいって
はきます	wear (bottom half)	はいて
はしります	run	はしって
はなします	speak/talk	はなして
ひきます	play music (string instruments)	ひいて
まちます	wait	まって
もちます	carry/hold	もって
よみます	read	よんで

Group 2 verbs

ます form	English	て form
あけます	open	あけて
おぼえます	remember	おぼえて
かぞえます	count	かぞえて
しめます	close	しめて
食べます	eat	食べて
つづけます	continue	つづけて
でかけます	go out	でかけて
ねます	sleep	ねて
みせます	show	みせて
みます	see	みて

Group 3 (irregular) verbs

ます form	English	て form
きます	come	きて
します	do/play sports	して

! 行きます is an exception.

07

八十七

Oh My Darling, て Forms!

To remember the rules for changing the ます form into the て form for Group 1 verbs and Group 3 (irregular) verbs (きます, します and 行きます), try learning this song. (Sung to the tune of *Oh My Darling, Clementine*.)

Verse 1

Uh my students,
Oh my students,
て is such a crazy form,
If you remember only
Group One,
you will never go wrong.

Verse 2

い、ち、り	→っし
ひ、み、に	→んで
き	→いて
ぎ	→いで
きます	→きて
します	→して
行きます	→行って

Counters

There are counters in English and in Japanese. For example, in English, we say 'three head of cattle', 'six people' or 'ten glasses of water'. In Japanese you need to use different counters depending on what you are talking about. You already know the counter for people (人), for example, 六人 .

In this unit, counters which can be used in general situations are introduced. However, there are a number of counters for specific situations as well. はい is one example. It is the counter for liquids served in glasses or cups, even for bowls of noodles!

You need to be careful with the pronunciation of counters because when they are written in kanji, you can't always tell how they should be said. The numbers with unexpected pronunciations are:

❶いっぱい　❸さんばい　❻ろっぱい　❽はっぱい　❿じゅっぱい

Particles make all the difference!

何に　しますか。　What have you decided on?

This phrase is used when people are deciding what they will order to eat. Make sure you use に and not を because the meaning of the sentence will change (see below).

A. 何に　しますか。
　　What have you decided upon?

A. 何を　しますか。
　　What do you do?

B. すしに　します。
　　I've decided on the sushi.

B. すしを　食べます。
　　I eat sushi.

八十八

カリフォルニアロールをつくろう!!!

ざいりょう (4人分)

のり	2まい
こめ	2はい
す	1/3 カップ
さとう 大きい スプーン	4 はい
しお 大きい スプーン	1ぱい
アボカド	1こ
きゅうり	1本
かにかまぼこ	100 グラム
マヨネーズ	すこし
しょうゆ	すこし
わさび	すこし

1. あたたかい ごはんに すと さとうと しおを まぜます。 ちょっと まちます。(10分)
2. アボカドと きゅうりを きります。
3. まきす (すしマット) の 上に のりを のせます。
4. のりの 上に ごはんと アボカドと きゅうりと かにかまぼこと マヨネーズを のせます。
5. まきましょう。
6. きりましょう。

できました!

! Some non-Japanese people think that Japanese people always eat sushi and sashimi, but Japanese cuisine is more than just sushi and sashimi! Research some foods that Japanese people eat every day or that are popular in Japan. Find a recipe for one of them and have a try at cooking it. Share your recipe with the class and write a review of the dish you made.

07

八十九

日本の おかし

春の おかし

夏の おかし

秋の おかし

冬の おかし

! There are a variety of traditional sweets in Japan.
They aren't always as 'sweet' as you'd expect.
Often, these sweets are eaten at tea ceremonies.
The shapes, patterns and colours of the sweets are
designed to represent the seasons.

Long and cylindrical items

いっぽん 一本
にほん 二本
さんぼん 三本
よんほん 四本
ごほん 五本
ろっぽん 六本
ななほん 七本
はっぽん 八本
きゅうほん 九　本
じゅっぽん 十　本
なんぼん 何本？

Thin and flat items

いちまい 一枚
にまい 二枚
さんまい 三枚
よんまい 四枚
ごまい 五枚
ろくまい 六枚
ななまい 七枚
はちまい 八枚
きゅうまい 九　枚
じゅうまい 十　枚
なんまい 何枚？

Floors in buildings

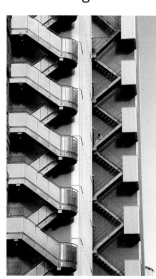

いっかい 一階
にかい 二階
さんがい 三階
よんかい 四階
ごかい 五階
ろっかい 六階
ななかい 七階
はちかい 八階
きゅうかい 九　階
じゅっかい 十　階
なんがい 何階？

Small animals

いっぴき 一匹
にひき 二匹
さんびき 三匹
よんひき 四匹
ごひき 五匹
ろっぴき 六匹
ななひき 七匹
はっぴき 八匹
きゅうひき 九　匹
じゅっぴき 十　匹
なんびき 何匹？

Books and magazines

いっさつ 一冊
にさつ 二冊
さんさつ 三冊
よんさつ 四冊
ごさつ 五冊
ろくさつ 六冊
ななさつ 七冊
はっさつ 八冊
きゅうさつ 九　冊
じゅっさつ 十　冊
なんさつ 何冊？

Houses and shops

いっけん 一軒
にけん 二軒
さんげん 三軒
よんけん 四軒
ごけん 五軒
ろっけん 六軒
ななけん 七軒
はっけん 八軒
きゅうけん 九　軒
じゅっけん 十　軒
なんげん 何軒？

Large animals

いっとう 一頭
にとう 二頭
さんとう 三頭
よんとう 四頭
ごとう 五頭
ろくとう 六頭
ななとう 七頭
はっとう 八頭
きゅうとう 九　頭
じゅっとう 十　頭
なんとう 何頭？

Machinery

いちだい 一台
にだい 二台
さんだい 三台
よんだい 四台
ごだい 五台
ろくだい 六台
ななだい 七台
はちだい 八台
きゅうだい 九　台
じゅうだい 十　台
なんだい 何台？

! Japanese has many special words for counting items. Different counters are used depending on the various characteristics of the items, such as their shape or size.

! Can you guess which counters should be used when counting the following things? うし (cows), パンや (bakeries), きんぎょ (goldfish), Tシャツ (T-shirts), ペン (pens), じしょ (dictionaries), CDプレーヤー (CD players).

おはしの　もちかた

Holding your chopsticks

Hold your chopsticks towards the thicker end. Rest the bottom chopstick on your fourth finger. Rest the top chopstick between your third finger and your forefinger. Place your thumb across both chopsticks.

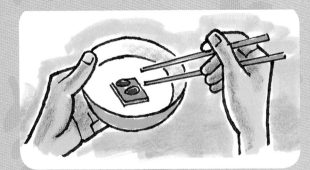

おはしの　うごかしかた

To move the top chopstick upwards, hold the bottom chopstick still and push your middle finger up.

To move the chopstick downwards, push the top chopstick down with your forefinger. Make sure there is a reasonable angle between the chopsticks at the thick end. You can pick up small items using this technique.

おわんの　もちかた

Holding your bowl

When drinking soup or eating rice, it is an important point of etiquette to pick up your bowl. In Japan, it is not considered rude if you slurp your food.

わるい　マナー

まよい　ばし

When you can't decide what you want to eat, don't wave your chopsticks around over the food.

さしばし

Don't stab food with your chopsticks.

よせばし

Don't pull the dishes towards you using your chopsticks. Always pick up the dish.

Don't pass food from one person to another with your chopsticks.

Don't leave your chopsticks stuck in your rice.

08

こうかん
りゅうがくせい

In this unit, you will learn to:

ask for and give permission to do something

refuse permission to do something

ask someone to do something for you and respond when asked

ask the reason why and respond when asked

recognise and write the kanji characters: 私，男，女，書，見，聞，父，母

In this unit, you will learn about:

Japanese etiquette and social customs

similarities and differences between school rules in Japan and Australia

cultural features of living in a Japanese home

being an exchange student in Japan

Jessica has just arrived in Japan on a short-term exchange programme. She is sending e-mails to her Japanese friends back home, letting them know what her new lifestyle is like.

ジェシカの Eメール

みなさん、こんにちは。私は 日本に います。日本は すばらしいです。
私の ホストファミリーは とても しんせつです。三人 かぞくです。
お父さんは かいしゃいんで とても いそがしいです。でも、 水えいが
大すきですから、 この しゅうまつに いっしょに うみに 行きます。
お母さんは やさしくて 日本ごを ゆっくり はなします。おねえさんも
高校 一年生ですから あした いっしょに 学校に 行きます。たのしみに
しています。
じゃ、また あした、学校の あとで、Eメールを 書きます。おやすみなさい。
ジェシカ

amazing

company employee

Questions

1 Who is in Jessica's new family?

2 How does she interact with each of them?

3 How does she feel about school?

Mother: ジェシカさん、 げんかんで くつを ぬいでください。それから
げたばこに いれて スリッパを はいてください。

Jessica: はい、 わかりました。

Mother: ジェシカさん、 この へやは わしつです。たたみの
へやです。 スリッパを ぬいでください。 このかべは
しょうじです。 しずかに あけてください。

Jessica: はい、 わかりました。お母さん、 ともだちに Eメールを
書きたいです。 コンピューターを つかっても いいですか。

Mother: はい、 どうぞ。ジェシカさんの へや コンピューターが あります。

Mother: ジェシカさん、 この へやは ジェシカさんの へやです。
おふろばは となりです。 いつでも シャワーを あびてください。

Jessica: ありがとう。 わあ、 まどから 小さい こうえんが 見えます。
行っても いいですか。

Mother: はい、 ばんごはんの あとで 行きましょう。

wall

paper door

bathroom/anytime
window

Questions

1 What places around the house did Jessica's host mother show her?

2 What is Jessica allowed to do?

3 When must Jessica be careful?

4 What activities does she have planned for the rest of the day?

08

九十四

the first time

really nervous

for example

of course

reply

みなさん、 きょうは　はじめて　学校に　行きました。 じてんしゃで
行きました。 ほんとうに　ドキドキしました。

私の　クラスメートは　みんな　やさしいですから　うれしいです。 男のこも
女のこも　います。

学校の　こうそくは　ちょっと　きびしいです。 たとえば、 きょうしつの
中で　MP3を　聞いては　だめです。 けいたいでんわも　つかっては
だめです。 ガムを　かんでは　だめです。 それから、 じゅぎょう中に
ともだちと　しゃべっては　だめです。 もちろん　ちこくしては　だめです。
それから、 おひるごはんを　こうていで　食べては　だめです。 へんですね。
みんな　きょうしつで　ひるごはんを　食べます。

じゃ、 つかれていますから、 もう　ねます。

へんじを　書いてくださいね。

ジェシカ

Questions

1 How did Jessica feel going to school? Why?

2 How does she describe her class?

3 What are some of the things the students are not allowed to do?

ジェシカの一日

ジェシカさん、 もう　七時半ですよ。
おきてください。 あさごはんの　前に
手と　かおを　あらってくださいね。
きょうは　さむいですから　ジャケットを
きてくださいね。 この　おべんとうは
かばんに　いれてください。

いただきます。

ごちそうさま。

いってらっしゃい。　いってきます。

おかえりなさい。

ただいま。

08

Questions

1 How is Jessica's host mother taking care of her?

2 When does Jessica use set phrases?

九十五

95

れんしゅう 🎵

01 Asking for and giving permission to do something

一 でんわを　つかっても　いいですか。
　　はい、いいです。

二 手を　あらっても　いいですか。
　　どうぞ。おふろばで　あらってください。

三 すみません。いま　シャワーを　あびても
　　いいですか。
　　はい、どうぞ。

02 Asking for and refusing permission to do something

一 せんせい、こうていで　おべんとうを
　　食べても　いいですか。
　　いいえ、きょうしつで　食べてください。

二 お母さん、そとで　ともだちと　あそんでも
　　いいですか。
　　だめです。へやを　そうじしてください。

03 Asking someone to do something for you and responding when asked

一 あさごはんの　前に　手を　あらってください。
　　はい。

二 ほうかご　買いものに　行ってください。
　　はい、行きます。

三 きたないですから　へやを　そうじしてください。
　　はい、わかりました。

04 Asking the reason why and responding

一 なぜ　はなしては　だめですか。
　　じゅぎょう中ですから。

二 なぜ　コンピューターを　つかっていますか。
　　Eメールを　書きたいですから。

三 なぜ　みんなと　いっしょに　パーティーに
　　行きませんでしたか。
　　そぼの　うちに　行きましたから、
　　行けませんでした。

漢字

かんじ

These are the kanji and their readings introduced in this unit.

わたし（わたくし）／シ　I/me

Someone pointing to their nose and saying 'me'.

ノ 二 千 千 禾 私 私

私の　→　わたしの　→　my/mine
私たち　→　わたしたち　→　we
私立学校　→　しりつがっこう　→　private school

おとこ　male/man

A man working in the rice field.

丨 冂 冂 Ⅲ 用 田 罗 男

男の人　→　おとこの　ひと　→　man
男の子　→　おとこの　こ　→　boy

おんな　female/woman

A woman wearing a kimono.

く 女 女

女の人　→　おんなの　ひと　→　woman
女の子　→　おんなの　こ　→　girl

か（きます）／ショ　to write

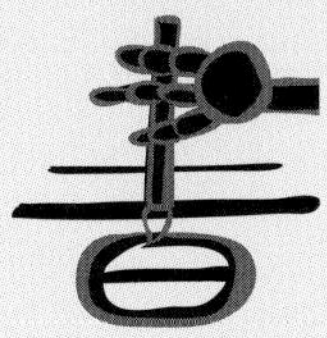

A hand holding a brush writing the kanji にち.

フ ユ ヨ ヨ ヨ 丰 聿 書 書 書

本を　書きます。→　ほんを　かきます。→　I will write a book.
書いています。→　かいています。→　I am writing.
書道　→　しょどう　→　calligraphy
辞書　→　じしょ　→　dictionary

08

九十七

かんじ

These are the kanji and their readings introduced in this unit.

み（ます）　to look/to see

An eye on legs moving around.

一	冂	冃	月	目	貝	見

テレビを　見ます。→　テレビを　みます。→　I will watch TV.
見えます。→　みえます。→　I can see (it).
見せます。→　みせます。→　I will show (it).

き（きます）／ブン　to listen/to hear

An ear listening to the loud speakers.

一	冂	冂	尸	尸	門	門	門
門	門	門	門	聞	聞		

CDを　聞きます。→　CDを　ききます。→　I will listen to a CD.
聞こえます。→　きこえます。→　I can hear.
聞いています。→　きいています。→　I am listening.
新聞　→　しんぶん　→　newspaper

ちち／（お）とう（さん）　father/dad

A man with broad shoulders.

ノ	ハ	父	父			

お父さん　→　おとうさん　→　father/dad
父　→　ちち　→　my father

はは／（お）かあ（さん）　mother/mum

A woman in a coat with big buttons.

乚	口	口	母	母		

お母さん　→　おかあさん　→　mother/mum
母　→　はは　→　my mother

ぶんぽう

Asking for permission

ばんごはんの　あとで　テレビを　見ても
いいですか。
May I watch TV after dinner?

じゅぎょう中に　けいたいでんわを
つかっても　いいですか。
Can I use a mobile phone during lessons.

Giving permission

はい、いいです。
Yes, you may.

Refusing permission

いいえ、じゅぎょう中に　つかっては　だめです。
No, you must not use it during lessons.

Asking someone to do something for you

みなさん、きょうしつを　そうじしてください。
Everyone, please clean the classroom.

Responding

はい、わかりました。
Yes, we will (we understood your request).

Asking for a reason

うちで　くつを　はいては　だめです。なぜですか。
Why can't we wear shoes in the house?

なぜ　ほうかご　買いものに　行きますか。
Why are you going shopping after school?

なぜ　テレビを　見ませんでしたか。
Why didn't you watch TV?

Giving a reason

きたないですから、うちで　くつを　はいては　だめです。
We don't wear shoes in the home because it is dirty.

あたらしい　せいふくを　買いたいですから、　買いものに　行きます。
I will go shopping because I want to buy a new uniform.

しゅくだいを　しましたから、テレビが　見られませんでした。
I couldn't watch TV because I did my homework.

08

たんご

Places

きょうしつ	classroom
げんかん	entrance
こうてい	school yard
たたみの　へや（わしつ）	tatami room

Verbs

あらいます	to wash
いれます	to put in
おきます	to get up
おふろに　はいります	to have a bath
かみます	to chew
さわります	to touch
しゃべります	to chat
シャワーを　あびます	to have a shower
そうじします	to clean
ちこくします	to be late
つかいます	to use
つかれます	to be tired
ドキドキします	to be nervous/excited
ぬぎます	to take off clothing
ねます	to sleep
はいります	to enter

Adjectives

あぶない	dangerous
うるさい	noisy
うれしい	happy
きたない	dirty
しんせつ（な）	kind
わかい	young

Phrases

いただきます。	I accept the meal/drink (before eating).
いってきます。	I'll be back.
いってらっしゃい	See you when you get back.
おかえりなさい。	Welcome home.
ごちそうさま。	Thank you for the meal/drink (after eating).
ごめんなさい。	I'm sorry.
しつれいします。	Excuse me/Goodbye.
すみません。	I'm sorry/Excuse me/Thank you.
ただいま。	I'm home.

Nouns

アクセサリー	accessories/jewellery
かばん	bag
きそく	rules
けいたいでんわ	mobile phone
けしょう	make-up
げたばこ/くつばこ	shoe box
こうそく	school rules
ごみ	rubbish
ごみばこ	rubbish bin
せいふく	uniform
ピアス	piercing
マニキュア	manicure/nail polish
らくがき	graffiti

School related words

じゅぎょう	lessons
じゅぎょう中	during lessons
ほうかご	after school

ぶんぽう Plus

Have you noticed in this unit that the て form can be used for so many things. Look at your choices:

食べて…	I eat AND ... (do something else)
食べています。	I am eating.
食べても　いいです。	I am allowed to eat.
食べては　だめです。	I'm not allowed to eat.
食べてください。	Please eat.

Once you have made the て form you just choose the ending you need to express what you want to say. Don't forget the little song that helps you make the て form (refer to page 88).

Watch out when using the word for BECAUSE – から.

It can be tricky so, for the moment, stick to the ways you have learnt in this unit.

After です

私は　日本ごが　すきですから、日本に　行きたいです。
高いですから、買いません。
きょうは　いい　てんきですから、こうえんに　行きましょう。

After ます／ました verbs

しゅくだいを　しましたから、テレビを　見ても　いいですか。

Before and After

You have learnt the words 前 (before) and あと (after). These are very useful. For example:

あさごはんの　前 (before breakfast)
ばんごはんの　あと (after dinner)

> ! There is a special word for after school: ほうかご.

How many other examples can you think of?

08

百一

エクストラ

Here is a list of rules Jessica saw on a poster on the classroom wall in her new school. In what way are the rules the same or different from your school rules?

こうそく

1 わるい　ことばを　つかっては　だめです。
2 学校で　ガムを　かんでは　だめです。
3 ごみを　ごみばこに　いれてください。
4 つくえと　かべに　らくがきを　しては　だめです。
5 ひるごはんを　きょうしつで　食べても　いいです。
6 けいたいでんわを　きょうしつで　つかっては　だめです。
7 まい日　しゅくだいを　してください。
8 けしょう、マニキュア、アクセサリーを　しては　だめです。
9 ちこくしては　だめです。

word

rubbish

wall

! Prepare a list of your school's rules to help a visiting exchange student.

Jessica's Japanese home has a わしつ – a Japanese-style room. Her host mother explained the rules of living in a Japanese home. What has she learned about her host family and their lifestyle?

- げんかんで　くつを　ぬいでください。
- しょうじは　かみですから、しずかに　あけてください。
- とこのまに　はいっては　だめです。
- ざぶとんの　上に　たっては　だめです。
- こたつは　ヒーターですから、きを　つけてください。
- トイレでは　トイレの　スリッパを　はいてください。

Imagine you have a Japanese student in your home. What would be your rules? Talk about shower and bath times, using the computer, TV, and about cleaning rooms. Make a list of rules – things you are allowed to do, not allowed to do and requests your mum and dad might make of you.

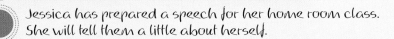

Jessica has prepared a speech for her home room class.
She will tell them a little about herself.

Jessica's speech

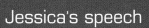

はじめまして。　私は　ジェシカ・テイラーです。　オーストラリア人です。　せん月
日本に　きました。　私は　ブリズベンに　すんでいます。　かぞくは　五人です。
父と　母と　あにが　二人　います。

私は　十年生です。　すきな　かもくは　ちりと　すうがくと　日本ごです。
しゅうまつに　ともだちと　うみに　でかけます。　私の　うちは　うみに
ちかいですから、　よく　うみで　水えいを　します。　みなさん、日本では
わかい　人は　しゅうまつに　何を　しますか。　おしえてください。

teach, tell

even, as well

日本の　食べものは　とても　おいしいです。　オーストラリアでも　日本の　食べものが
買えますから、　母と　よく　日本りょうりを　つくります。　私の　一ばん　すきな

handrolled sushi

りょうりは　手まきずしです。　いっしょに　つくりましょう。　私の　ホストの
お母さんは　りょうりが　上手ですから、　まい日　ばんごはんが　たのしみです。　私の
ホストファミリーは　とても　しんせつです。

日本の　学校の　きそくは　きびしいです。　この　学校は　大きいです。　それから

first/nervous

せいとが　たくさん　います。　さいしょは　ちょっと　ドキドキしました。
でも　みなさん　とても　やさしいです。　ともだちが　たくさん　できましたから、
うれしいです。

**culture/as hard as
I can**

日本ごと　日本の　ぶんかを　いっしょうけんめい　べんきょうします。

What information does
Jessica give about herself?
Write a profile of yourself in
preparation for introducing
yourself to Japanese people
you might meet at school or
in Japan.

08

百
三

ともだちの　プロフィール

Survey a friend. Ask them these questions and write their answers in your exercise book.

1 おなまえは?

2 何時に　おきますか。

3 学校の　前に　何を　しますか。

4 学校の　あとで　ともだちと　何を　しますか。

5 何で　学校に　行きますか。

6 学校で　何を　べんきょうしていますか。

7 一ばん　すきな　おんがくは　何ですか。

8 しゅうまつに　何を　しますか。

9 うちで　くつを　はいていますか。

10 うちで　コンピューターを　つかいますか。

> ! だれでしょうか。Draw up a chart of five or six questions and survey a class member. Report back to the class without saying who you are talking about and see if the rest of the class can identify who it is.

ビンゴゲーム

Choose a square. Translate correctly and put an object on top to claim the box as yours.

Three correct answers in a row wins the game. Put the Japanese into English or the English into Japanese as necessary.

We must not eat in the classroom.	ともだちは みんな やさしいですから うれしいです。	Please write your name in Japanese.	きょうしつで じゅぎょう中に ともだちと しゃべっては だめです。
ほうかご でんしゃで まちへ　一人で 行っても いいです。	Because it is hot I will go to the beach today.	らい年 留学生に なりたいです。	We are allowed to play soccer in the school yard.
I want to buy new shoes this week.	あしたは　テストが ありますから　きょう べんきょうして ください。	I am talking to my friend on the phone.	かんじが よめませんから ひらがなで 書いても いいです。

08

百四

09

まっすぐ行きます

In this unit, you will learn to:

ask where something is

give directions

say when/if you do something and what happens next

join two or more sets of actions

use the structure てから

ask how long it takes to go somewhere or to do something and respond

recognise and write the kanji characters: 左, 右, 入, 出, 南, 北, 西, 東

In this unit, you will learn about:

the similarities and differences of towns in Japan and Australia

Japanese conversation strategies

セーラと　しょうこ

Comic by Yuko Fujita

セーラさん、
らいしゅうの　土曜日に　やさかじんじゃで　おまつりが
あります。いっしょに　行きませんか。ホストシスターの
しょうこさんと　きてください。ごご　三時に
やさかじんじゃで　あいましょう。
しんたろうより

じんじゃで
おまつり！
たのしみ！

きょうと、きょうと、
きょうとです。
ドアが　しまります。

大きい　えき！

セーラさん、
しんたろうくんの
てがみを　みせてください。

えーと、西口は
出てから　右。

タクシーのりば
北こうばん
トイレ
バスてい
ホテルグランヴィア
プラットフォーム
デパート
？
ゆうびんきょく
西口
東京→
しんかんせん 東口
トイレ
←おおさか
しんかんせん 中央口

すみません。
西口は　どこですか。

西口ですか。
あの　かいだんの
上です。

09

百六

ドアが　しまります。.....The door is closing.　　かいだん.....................stairs

あのかいだんの
上ですね。
ありがとう
ございます。

あ、西口が
ありました。西口を
出てから、右。

そうすると、バスていが
あります。あ、バスていが
ありましたよ。

しょうこさん、
トイレに
行きたいです。

えっ。
トイレですか。
セーラさん、
ちょっと
まってください。

すみません。
この　へんに
トイレが
ありますか。

トイレですか。はい、ありますよ。
デパートの　かどを　左に
まがってください。そうすると、
ゆうびんきょくが　あります。
トイレは　ゆうびんきょくの
中に　ありますよ。

つぎは　しじょうかわらまち、
しじょうかわらまちです。

わあー。大きい
デパートが
たくさん
あります。

ゆうびんきょくの
中ですね。
ありがとう。

すみません。
やさかじんじゃに
行きたいんですが…

やさかじんじゃですか。ええと…この
みちを　まっすぐ　行きます。そうすると、
はしが　あります。その　はしを　わたって、
ずっと　まっすぐ　行きます。そうすると、
やさかじんじゃが　ありますよ。

この　みちを
まっすぐですね。
そして、はしを
わたって、ずっと
まっすぐですね。
わかりました。

そうですね。
あるいて　五分ぐらいです。
とおくないですよ。

すみません。
ここから
じんじゃまで
どのぐらい　かかりますか。

そうですか。
ありがとう
ございました。

セーラさん、
もうすぐですよ。
この　みちを
まっすぐです。

しょうこさん、あついですね。
アイスクリームを　食べたいですね。

すみません。
この　へんに
きっさてんが
ありますか。

はい、ありますよ。
この　しんごうを
左に　まがって
ください。
右がわに
きっさてんが
ありますよ。

しょうこさん、
はやく！しんごうが
あおです。左に
まがって！しんごうを
わたって！

セーラ！

ずっと .... all the way
もうすぐ .... very soon
しんごうが　あおです。 . The traffic
　　　　　　　　　　　light is green.

Questions

1　What is the relationship between Shoko and Sarah?
2　When is the festival? What time and where are they meeting?
3　Which exit do they have to take? Where do they have to go after that?
4　How long does it take to get to Shijo-Kawaramachi?
5　Where did Sarah want to go? Where is it?
6　What are the three different ways to ask directions?
7　How do they get to Yasaka shrine? Is it far from where they are?
8　Where does Sarah want to go now? And where is it?
9　What happened in the end?

練習
れんしゅう

01 Asking where something is and responding

一　すみません。ぎんこうは　どこですか。
　　ぎんこうですか。ぎんこうは　えきの　前に　あります。

二　すみません。この　へんに　トイレは　ありますか。
　　トイレですか。トイレは　としょかんの　中に　あります。

三　すみません。としょかんに　行きたいんですが…
　　としょかんですか。としょかんは　こうえんの　となりに　あります。

02 Giving directions

一　この　みちを　まっすぐ　行きます。
二　その　はしを　わたります。
三　あの　しんごうを　右に　まがります。
四　ぎんこうの　かどを　左に　まがります。
五　二つめの　かどを　右に　まがります。
六　そうすると、ぎんこうは　右がわに　あります。

03 Joining two or more sets of actions

一　この　こうさてんを　まっすぐ　行って、つぎの　しんごうを　右に　まがります。
二　その　しんごうを　わたって、まっすぐ　行ってください。
三　あの　かどを　右に　まがって、まっすぐ　行って、コンビニの　かどを　左に　まがります。そうすると、大きい　こうえんが　あります。

04 Saying two or more sets of actions emphasising the order of the actions

一　はしを　わたってから　右に　まがります。
二　学校の　あと、ゆうびんきょくに　行ってから、うちに　かえります。
三　しゅくだいを　してから　テレビを　見ます。

05 Asking how long it takes and responding

一　どのぐらい　かかりますか。
　　あるいて　十分ぐらい　かかります。ちかいですよ。

二　うちから　学校まで　どのぐらい　かかりますか。
　　でんしゃで　五十分ぐらい　かかります。ちょっと　とおいです。

三　しゅくだいは　どのぐらい　かかりましたか。
　　日本ごの　しゅくだいは　二十分ぐらい　かかりました。

These are the kanji and their readings introduced in this unit.

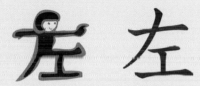 左

When you see a horizontal 'l,' turn left.

一 ナ ナ 左 左

左に　まがります。　→　ひだりに　まがります。　→　I will turn left.
左がわ　→　ひだりがわ　→　left-hand side
左手　→　ひだりて　→　left hand

 右

The man says, 'I'm right.'

ノ ナ ナ 右 右

右に　まがります。→　みぎに　まがります。→　I will turn right.
右がわ　→　みぎがわ　→　right-hand side
右目　→　みぎめ　→　right eye
左右　→　さゆう　→　left and right

  入

A person entering a room.

ノ 入

入ります。　→　はいります。　→　I will enter.
入口　→　いりぐち　→　entrance
入学　→　にゅうがく　→　entering school

 出

A volcano with two mountains exploding.

| 十 中 出 出

出ます。→　でます。→　I will leave.
出口　→　でぐち　→　exit
出かけます。　→　でかけます。→　I will go out.
出ぱつ　→　しゅっぱつ　→　departure

かんじ

These are the kanji and their readings introduced in this unit.

 みなみ／ナン **south**

Criminals bury some money under a hill.

一	十	广	古	市	市	両	南
南							

南	→	みなみ	→	south
南がわ	→	みなみがわ	→	south side
南口	→	みなみぐち	→	south entrance
南東	→	なんとう	→	south-east

 きた／ホク **north**

Which way is north? One says this way, one says that way.

一	十	土	北	北			

北	→	きた	→	north
北がわ	→	きたがわ	→	north side
北口	→	きたぐち	→	north entrance
北西	→	ほくせい	→	north-west

 にし／セイ **west**

Four wise men in the west invented pi.

一	丆	丙	丙	西	西		

西	→	にし	→	west
西がわ	→	にしがわ	→	western side
西口	→	にしぐち	→	western entrance
南西	→	なんせい	→	south-west

  ひがし／トウ **east**

The sun rises from behind a tree in the east.

一	丆	丙	戸	旦	車	東	東

東	→	ひがし	→	east
東がわ	→	ひがしがわ	→	eastern side
東口	→	ひがしぐち	→	eastern entrance
東北	→	とうほく	→	north-eastern district of Japan

09

百
十
一

Asking directions

すみません。えいがかんは　どこですか。
Excuse me. Where is the movie theatre?

この　へんに　トイレが　ありますか
Is there a toilet around here?

すみません。ゆうびんきょくに　行きたいんですが…
Excuse me. I want to go to the post office …

Giving directions

この　みちを　まっすぐ　行きます。
Go straight along this road.

しんごうを　わたります
Cross at the traffic light.

ぎんこうの　かどを　右に　まがります。
Turn right at the corner of the bank.

二つめの　かどを　左に　まがります。
Turn left at the second corner.

そうすると、パンやは　左がわに　あります。
When you do that, the bakery is on the left-hand side.

えいがかんは　えきの　前です。
The movie theatre is in front of the station.

Joining two or more sets of actions

この　みちを　まっすぐ　行って、つぎの　かどを　右に　まがります。
Go straight ahead on this road and turn right at the next corner.

Joining two or more sets of actions with emphasis on the order of the actions

えきを　出てから、しんごうを　わたります。
Go out of the station, and (after that) cross at the traffic light.

Asking how long it takes to get somewhere

うちから　学校まで　どのぐらい　かかりますか。
How long does it take from home to school?

Responding

うちから　学校まで　あるいて　十分ぐらい　かかります。
From home to school, it takes about 10 minutes on foot.

Place names

えいがかん	movie theatre
としょかん	library
びじゅつかん	art gallery
りょかん	Japanese-style inn
はなや	flower shop
にくや	butcher
本や	bookshop
やおや	greengrocer
くすりや	pharmacy
くつや	shoe shop
こうえん	park
えき	train station
パンや	bakery
ぎんこう	bank
ゆうびんきょく	post office
びょういん	hospital
おてら	Buddhist temple
スーパー	supermarket
じんじゃ	Shinto shrine
コンビニ	convenience store
デパート	department store
バスてい	bus stop
ホテル	hotel
タクシーのりば	taxi stand
ちかてつ	subway

Landmarks

入口	entrance
かど	corner
こうさてん	intersection
しんごう	traffic signal/lights
出口	exit
はし	bridge
みち	road

Other direction words

一つめ or 一ばんめ	first
二つめ or 二ばんめ	second
三つめ or 三ばんめ	third
つぎ	next
右	right
左	left
右がわ	right-hand side
左がわ	left-hand side
北	north
南	south
東	east
西	west

こ / そ / あ / ど

ここ	here (near the speaker)
そこ	there (near the listener)
あそこ	over there (away from both the speaker and listener)
どこ	where
このへん	around here

Verbs

かかります	to take time
出ます	to exit/leave
入ります	to enter
まっすぐ 行きます	to go straight
右に まがります	to turn right
わたります	to cross

Adjectives

ちかい	nearby/close
とおい	far

09

百十三

文法
ぶんぽう Plus

Do you remember この, その, あの and これ, それ, あれ in Unit 4? In this unit, ここ, そこ, あそこ and どこ have been introduced. Study the summary below.

Near the speaker

When an object is near the speaker use こ.

この + noun → この CD (this CD)
これ + particle → これを　ください。 (I'll have this one please.)
ここ → ここに　あります。 (It is here.)

Near the listener

When an object is near the listener use そ.

その + noun → その CD (that CD)
それ + particle → それは　きれいです。 (That one is pretty.)
そこ → そこに　あります。 (It is there.)

Far away from the speaker and listener

When an object is far away from the speaker and the listener use あ.

あの + noun → あの CD (that CD over there)
あれ + particle → あれが　食べたいです。 (I want to eat that one over there.)
あそこ → あそこです。 (It is over there.)

Question words

When you ask a question use ど.

どの + noun → どの CD (Which CD?)
どれ + particle → どれが　すきですか。 (Which one do you like?)
どこ → どこですか。 (Where is it?)

Asking directions

We have learned three different ways to ask directions.

1. きっさてんは　どこですか。 (Where is the coffee shop?)

2. この へんに きっさてんが ありますか。(Is there a coffee shop around here?)

3. きっさてんに　行きたいんですが… (I want to got to a coffee shop, but ...)

When you want to go to a coffee shop you can say きっさてんに 行きたいです。But by inserting ん, you emphasise your desire to go. By adding が to the end of a sentence you are inviting the listener to join the conversation. For example, 'I want to go to a coffee shop, but ...'

そうすると

そうすると (if/when you do that) is a useful phrase when you want to say something will happen as the result of an action. For example:

おんがくを　聞きます。そうすると、リラックスできます。
(I listen to music. If I do that, I can relax.)

エクストラ

Look at the map of Yusuke's home town, and compare it to your suburb. What are the differences and similarities?

Yusuke wrote down how to get to places from his house for his host brother, Alex. Read Yusuke's directions, and find his house. Yusuke is also a keen jogger. Read his jogging course outline and try to workout his route.

Using Yusuke's notes, write a similar note to a host brother or sister coming to stay with you.

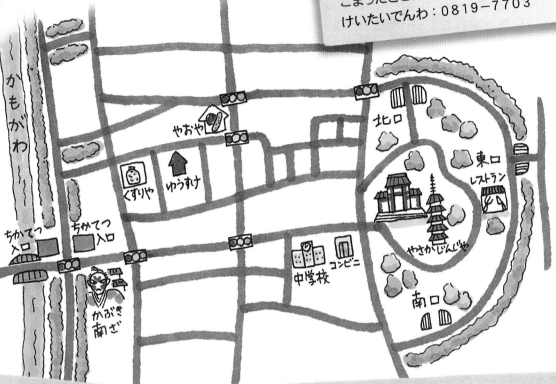

学校

うちを 出て 右に 行きます。そうすると、しんごうが あります。その しんごうを 右に まがります。そして、つぎの しんごうを 左に まがって、まっすぐ 行ってください。右がわに 中学校が あります。うちから 学校まで あるいて 五分です。

こまったときは でんわしてください。
けいたいでんわ：0819-7703

ぼくは まいあさ、ジョギングを します。うちを 出て、左に まがって まっすぐ 行きます。そうすると、かもがわが あります。かもがわでともだちの けんたくんに あいます。けんたくんと いっしょに かもがわの よこの みちを 左に まがって 一つめの しんごうを 左に まがります。そして、五分ぐらい まっすぐ 行きます。そうすると、右がわに 小さい コンビニが あります。その コンビニで オレンジジュースを 買って 飲みます。コンビニの ちかくに ふるい じんじゃが あります。その じんじゃの うしろに ひろい こうえんが あります。その こうえんで 十分くらい トレーニングを してから、こうえんを 出ます。こうえんの 北口を 出て、まっすぐ 行きます。二つめの しんごうを 左に まがって つぎの やおやの かどを 右に まがります。ぼくの うちは 左がわに あります。

ちかてつ のえき

うちを 出て 左に まっすぐ 行ってください。そして、くすりやの かどを 左に まがります。そうすると、しんごうが あります。しんごうを 右に まがってください。そうすると、ちかてつの 入口が あります。そこの しんごうを わたってから 入口に 入ります。うちから ちかてつの えきまで あるいて 三分です。べんりですね。

09

こまったときは ....when (you are) in trouble
ちかく ....near by

百十五

115

ゲームを　しましょう。

You can play this game with a partner or against another team.

- Take turns to nominate a category. For example,「かんじの　五　おねがいします」(Kanji for 5 points please).
- If you answer correctly, you receive the points allocated to the question.
- For はなしましょう, answer the questions in Japanese.
- You must answer within 30 seconds.

じゃあ、ゲームを　スタート！

Points	かんじ	たんご	ぶんぽう	はなしましょう
一	What does this kanji mean? 南	What does this word mean? ゆうびんきょく	Say 'From here to school.'	学校から　まちまで　どのくらい　かかりますか。
二	What do these kanji mean? 出口 and 入口	What is 'hospital' in Japanese?	Say 'Turn right at the corner of the bank.'	このへんに　トイレが　ありますか。どこですか。
三	How do you read these kanji? 北 and 西	Say 'the first', 'the second' and 'the third' in Japanese.	Ask where the coffee shop is in three different ways	この　へんに　コンビニが　ありますか。どこですか。
四	Write the kanji for 'east'	Say five place names in Japanese	Say 'Go straight and cross the bridge.'	うちから　学校まで　どのぐらい　かかりますか。
五	Write the kanji for ひだりて.	What are じんじゃ, おてら, やおや, びじゅつかん and こうさてん？	Say 'Do homework and after that, watch TV.'	えきの　前に　何が　ありますか。

スコア		
16-20	10-15	0-9
すごいですね。 Congratulations! You are the champion!	もうちょっと… Nearly there! Go over the questions that you got wrong.	がんばって！ Go over the ぶんぽう & たんご page. Good luck!

10

スポーツヒーロー

In this unit, you will learn to:

make the dictionary form of verbs

say that you like or dislike doing things

say that someone is good at or not good at doing something

say that you can, cannot, could or could not do something

conduct an interview in Japanese

recognise and write the kanji characters: 毎，今，週，先，来，住，好，名

In this unit, you will learn about:

the lifestyle of a trainee sumo wrestler

traditional and popular sports in Japan

Japanese Olympians

Ayumi is writing an article on an athlete for next week's edition of her school newspaper. She is doing an interview via an Internet chat room for the article.

インタビュー

Ayumi: こんにちは。お名前は何ですか。

Hideki: 高見ひできです。

A: 学校しんぶんで、スポーツせんしゅについてのきじを書きたいんですが、インタビューしてもいいですか。

H: はい、いいですよ。

A: ひできさんはおいくつですか。

H: 十七さいです。

A: ひできさんはどんなスポーツが好きですか。

H: ぼくはすもうが大好きです。

A: どこに住んでいますか。

H: 東京のすもうべやに住んでいます。今年から、すもうべやでれんしゅうしています。

A: そうですか。何年かんすもうをしていますか。

H: 八年かんぐらいしています。ぼくはこどもの時から、テレビですもうを見ることが好きでした。つよくてゆうめいなりきしによくあこがれました。

A: れんしゅうはどうですか。どのぐらいれんしゅうしますか。

H: 毎日六時かんぐらいれんしゅうします。れんしゅうはとてもきびしいですよ。毎日ごぜん六時から十二時までれんしゅうします。

A: じゃあ、ごごは何をしますか。

H: ひるねをします。それから、本をよみます。テレビも見ます。六時ごろにばんごはんを食べます。

---

an article about athletes

How old are you?

sumo

sumo training stable

How many years?
since I was a child
I often admired sumo wrestlers.

nap

10

百
十
八

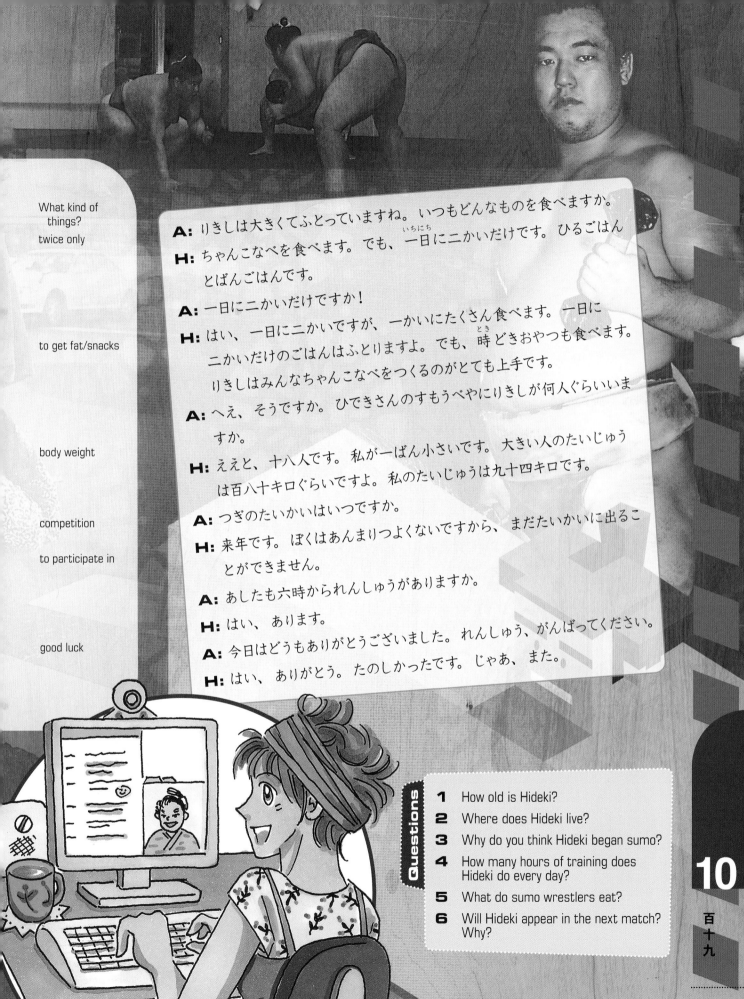

What kind of things?
twice only

to get fat/snacks

body weight

competition

to participate in

good luck

A: りきしは大きくてふとっていますね。いつもどんなものを食べますか。

H: ちゃんこなべを食べます。でも、一日に二かいだけです。ひるごはん とばんごはんです。

A: 一日に二かいだけですか！

H: はい、一日に二かいですが、一かいにたくさん食べます。一日に 二かいだけのごはんはふとりますよ。でも、時どきおやつも食べます。 りきしはみんなちゃんこなべをつくるのがとても上手です。

A: へえ、そうですか。ひできさんのすもうべやにりきしが何人ぐらいいま すか。

H: ええと、十八人です。私が一ばん小さいです。大きい人のたいじゅう は百八十キロぐらいですよ。私のたいじゅうは九十四キロです。

A: つぎのたいかいはいつですか。

H: 来年です。ぼくはあんまりつよくないですから、まだたいかいに出るこ とができません。

A: あしたも六時かられんしゅうがありますか。

H: はい、あります。

A: 今日はどうもありがとうございました。れんしゅう、がんばってください。

H: はい、ありがとう。たのしかったです。じゃあ、また。

Questions

1 How old is Hideki?

2 Where does Hideki live?

3 Why do you think Hideki began sumo?

4 How many hours of training does Hideki do every day?

5 What do sumo wrestlers eat?

6 Will Hideki appear in the next match? Why?

10

百十九

練習
れんしゅう

01 Asking and saying what you like or dislike doing

一 うみでおよぐことが好きですか。
　 はい、およぐことが好きです。
二 すうがくをべんきょうすることが好きですか。
　 いいえ、好きじゃないです。
三 へやをそうじすることが好きですか。
　 いいえ、きらいです。私のへやはきたないです。
四 フットボールを見ることが好きですか。
　 はい、大好きです。よくテレビで見ます。

02 Asking and saying if a person is good at something

一 えみこさんはしゃしんをとることが上手ですか。
　 はい、しゃしんをとることが上手です。
二 先生は日本ごをおしえることが上手ですか。
　 はい、私の先生は日本ごをおしえることがとても上手です。
三 やきゅうが上手ですか。
　 いいえ、上手じゃないです。下手です。

03 Asking and saying what you can or cannot do

一 じてんしゃにのることができますか。
　 はい、じてんしゃにのることができます。
二 さしみを食べることができますか。
　 はい、さしみを食べることができます。
三 けんどうをすることができますか。
　 いいえ、けんどうをすることができません。
四 あした、ごぜん八時に来ることができますか。
　 すみません、あした八時に行くことができません。

10

百
二
十

120

かんじ

These are the kanji and their readings introduced in this unit.

 マイ every

Every day Mum puts on her hat.

ノ ― ― ― ― 毎

毎日	→	まいにち	→	every day
毎月	→	まいつき	→	every month
毎年	→	まいとし	→	every year
毎日しんぶんをよみます。	→	まいにちしんぶんをよみます。	→	I read the newspaper every day.

 **いま／コン** now/this

Who wants to eat now?

ノ 人 今 今

今から	→	いまから	→	from now
今日	→	きょう	→	today
今月	→	こんげつ	→	this month
今年	→	ことし	→	this year

 シュウ week

Which shoes will you wear this week?

ノ 刀 月 月 月 用 周 周
周 週 週

今週	→	こんしゅう	→	this week
先週	→	せんしゅう	→	last week
週まつ	→	しゅうまつ	→	weekend
毎週一かい	→	まいしゅういっかい	→	once a week

 セン previous

The teacher is holding a pen.

ノ ― 牛 生 先 先

先生	→	せんせい	→	teacher
先週	→	せんしゅう	→	last week
先月	→	せんげつ	→	last month
先日	→	せんじつ	→	the other day

10

百二十一

漢字

かんじ

These are the kanji and their readings introduced in this unit.

き(ます)／く／こ／ライ **to come/next**

 来

Birds sit on a tree branch.

一　一　一　一　平　来　来

来てください。	→	きてください。	→	Please come.
来週	→	らいしゅう	→	next week
来月	→	らいげつ	→	next month
来年	→	らいねん	→	next year

す(んでいます)／ジュウ **to live**

 住

The people live in a three-storey building with an antenna.

ノ　イ　イ　伫　件　住　住

住んでいます。	→	すんでいます。	→	I am living ...
住んでいました。	→	すんでいました。	→	I was living ...
京都に住んでいます。	→	きょうとにすんでいます。	→	I am living in Kyoto.
シドニーに住んでいます。	→	シドニーにすんでいます。	→	I am living in Sydney.

す(き) **to like**

 好

The mother loves her child.

く　く　女　女　好　好

好きな食べもの	→	すきなたべもの	→	the food I like
ケーキが好きです。	→	ケーキがすきです。	→	I like cake.
ゴルフが好きでした。	→	ゴルフがすきでした。	→	I used to like golf.
好きな人	→	すきなひと	→	the person I like

な／メイ **name**

 名

My name is タロ (Taro).

ノ　ク　タ　タ　名　名

名前	→	なまえ	→	name
名古屋	→	なごや	→	Nagoya
ゆう名な人	→	ゆうめいなひと	→	famous person
名人	→	めいじん	→	expert/master

10

百
二
十
二

Saying what you like or dislike doing

You can already say 'I like basketball' in Japanese: バスケットボールが好きです. Here you will learn how to say things like 'I like playing basketball' or 'I don't like watching basketball'. The plain (dictionary) form of verbs is used in this pattern. For more information about this verb form refer to 文法 Plus.

すもうを　見る　ことが　好きです。
I like watching sumo.

まんがを　よむ　ことが　好きでした。
I liked reading/to read comics.

カラオケバーで　うたう　のが　きらいです。
I don't like singing at karaoke bars.

Saying if a person is good or not good at something

In general, this pattern is used to say someone is good at or not good at something, or not good at doing an activity. The plain form of verbs is also used for this pattern.

ジェニーさんは　ピアノを　ひく　のが　下手です。
Jenny is not good at playing the piano.

たかはしさんは　人の前で　はなす　ことが　上手です。
Mr Takahashi is good at speaking in front of people.

私は　えを　かく　のが　下手でした。
I was not good at drawing pictures.

Saying what you can, cannot, could or could not do

You can say you can or cannot do an action by using the potential verb forms. For example, 書けます (I can write) or 出かけられません (I can't go out).

You can also say you could or couldn't do an action by using the past tense. For example, 書けました (I could write) or 出かけられませんでした (I couldn't go out).

Here is another way of saying you can or cannot do an action. You might wonder why there are two ways of saying the same thing. Good point! This allows you to vary your language and avoid repetition.

1. 日本の　しんぶんを　よむ　ことが　できます。
2. 日本の　しんぶんが　よめます。
I can read a Japanese newspaper.

1. キムさんは　ノートを　見つける　ことが　できません。
2. キムさんは　ノートが　見つけられません。
Kim can't find her notebook.

1. ひろふみくんは　カラオケパーティーに　来る　ことが　できました。
2. ひろふみくんは　カラオケパーティーに　来られました。
Hirofumi could come to the karaoke party.

1. ひできさんは　しあいに　かつ　ことが　できませんでした。

2. ひできさんは　しあいに　かてませんでした。
Hideki couldn't win the match.

! You can't use this pattern for expressions like 'I am good at getting up in the morning'.

10
百二十三

123

たんご

The dictionary form of verbs

Group 1 verbs

ます form	English	Dictionary form
あいます	meet	あう
あらいます	wash	あらう
およぎます	swim	およぐ
おわります	finish	おわる
かえります	return	かえる
かちます	win	かつ
がんばります	try hard	がんばる
聞きます	listen	きく
きります	cut	きる
すわります	sit	すわる
たちます	stand up	たつ
つかいます	use	つかう
つくります	make	つくる
のります	ride	のる
はしります	run	はしる
はなします	speak/talk	はなす
まちます	wait	まつ
もちます	carry/hold	もつ
入ります	enter	はいる

Group 2 verbs

ます form	English	Dictionary form
あけます	open	あける
おきます	get up, wake up	おきる
おしえます	teach	おしえる
おぼえます	remember	おぼえる
かぞえます	count	かぞえる
しめます	close	しめる
出ます	leave, participate, attend	でる
つけます	turn on, switch on	つける
つづけます	continue	つづける
まけます	lose	まける
見せます	show	みせる
見つけます	find	見つける
見ます	see	みる
やめます	quit	やめる

Group 3 (irregular) verbs

ます form	English	Dictionary form
きます	come	くる
うんてんします	drive	うんてんする
じゅんびします	prepare	じゅんびする
ジョギングします	jog	ジョギングする
そうじします	clean	そうじする
リラックスします	relax	リラックスする
れんしゅうします	practise	れんしゅうする

> ! You can use verbs you already know with the patterns from the 文法 page – just remember that they have to be in the plain form. Be careful to use the correct particles! For more verbs and a quick reference to the plain forms, refer to pages 166 to 167 at the back of the book.

10

ぶんぽう Plus

The plain (dictionary) form of verbs

You have seen several different verb forms so far: the polite (ます) form (e.g. うたいます), the て form (e.g. うたって), and the potential form (e.g. うたえます). In this unit, you will learn another verb form: the plain present or dictionary form.

The plain form is used in a variety of ways such as:

- in dictionaries
- in forming different grammatical patterns
- for less formal (friendly, casual) speech
- for informal writing (i.e. diary entries, newspapers and academic reports).

You may have seen examples of verbs used in the plain form previously.

Group One verbs

うたいます → うたう		to sing
よみます → よむ		to read
かえります → かえる		to return

Group Two verbs

あけます → あける		to open
食べます → 食べる		to eat
見ます → 見る		to see/watch

Group Three verbs (irregular)

来ます → 来る		to come
します → する		to do/play

Speaking or writing

Some of the patterns introduced in this unit offer more than one way of saying the same thing in Japanese. So is there a difference in their uses? Look at the following examples.

うたをうたう**こと**が好きです ＝ うたをうたう**の**が好きです

こと and の are interchangeable, but こと is used more often in written Japanese.

うたえます ＝ うたうことができます

うたえます is more common in speech, and うたうことができます is more often used in writing.

10

Sport in Japan

Investigate a traditional Japanese sport, researching its history, popularity inside and outside of Japan, its rules and skills and its famous players. Develop a class book, or website on traditional Japanese sports. Include information gained by talking to Japanese speakers and about their experiences whenever you can. Here are some ideas: kemari, kyudo and Japanese martial arts such as judo, kendo, sumo, aikido, and karate.

Popular Japanese sports

Research the types of sports that are popular as spectator sports and as participatory sports for people of different age groups in Japan. Present your findings in visual form using graphs, charts, pictures with captions etc., labelled in Japanese. Include information gained by interviewing or surveying in Japanese whenever you can.

インタビューを
しましょう!

Interviews are lots of fun because they give you the chance to use your Japanese in a real situation. One of the keys to a successful interview is careful preparation. Try to use as many different patterns as you can. Often the person is doing a favour for you, so show your appreciation at the beginning and the conclusion of the interview. You might like to record or film the interview. If so, you should seek permission from the interviewee before you start.

Preparation

Purpose:
- what do you want to find out?
- what can you do with the information you have gained?

Structure:
- prepare your questions in Japanese before the interview
- prepare vocabulary you think may be used in the responses and check that you are clear about meaning.

Asking permission to conduct the interview:

- すみません。すこし時かんがありますか。
  Excuse me, can you spare some time?
- すこしいいですか。
  Do you have a few spare moments?
- インタビューをしてもいいですか。
  May I interview you?
- ～についてインタビューをしているんですが…
  I am conducting an interview about …
- すみません。インタビューをろくおんしてもいいですか。
  Excuse me, may I record the interview?

Keeping the conversation flowing

あいづち (listener responses) are important features in a Japanese conversation because they keep the conversation flowing. They indicate the listener is listening to the speaker. They also offer polite encouragement. Practise using あいづち when you talk in Japanese. Here are some you could use.

はい。	Yes.
うん。	Yes. (casual)
はい、はい。	Yes, go on.
へえ!	Wow! (casual)
ふうん。	I see. (casual)
わあ。	Wow! (casual)
ほんとうですか?	Really?
すごいですね!	Isn't it great?
そうですね。	I think so.
ああ、そうですか。	Oh, is that so? (Often used when disagreeing.)

Key question words

おいくつですか。	How old are you?
何か	something/anything
何を	What?
どこで	Where?
いつから／何時に	When from/what time?
どうして／なぜ	Why?
だれが／だれと	Who?/Who with?
どのぐらい	About how long?
どちらが／どれが	Which one?
どんな〜	What kind of ...?

Showing your appreciation:

- きょうはどうもありがとうございました。
  Thank you very much for today.
- いろいろ聞かせていただいてありがとうございました。
  Thank you for telling us about all these things.

When you need the information repeated:

- もう一ど言ってください。
  Please repeat it.
- ゆっくり言ってください。
  Please speak more slowly.

メモをとりましょう！

Although you may be able to record or film the interview, it is always handy to be able to take notes. Note taking helps you to keep track of the information, alter your questions depending on the answers and to ask additional questions. It can also save time when you come to summarise the information.

The key is to take down information quickly and briefly (not too brief so that you can still understand what you have written when you read it later!) Take notes in Japanese rather than English. Jot down words or key phrases rather than whole sentences. But, most of all relax and have fun!

ちょうせん

Conduct an interview in Japanese with a person such as an exchange student, a visitor or a tourist. Think about the purpose of the interview and prepare your questions. While interviewing, take notes. Present an oral or written summary of the information you have gained from the interview. Ask your teacher for the assessment criteria.

10

オリンピック

夏のオリンピック

29 回目 北京オリンピック (2008) 　中国
28 回目 アテネオリンピック (2004) 　ギリシャ
27 回目 シドニーオリンピック (2000) 　オーストラリア
26 回目 アトランタオリンピック (1996) 　アメリカ

冬のオリンピック

20 回目 トリノオリンピック (2006) 　イタリア
19 回目 ソルトレイクシティーオリンピック (2002) アメリカ
18 回目 長野オリンピック (1998) 　日本
17 回目 リレハンメルオリンピック (1994) 　ノルウェー

日本でのオリンピック

1964 　東京オリンピック (夏)
1972 　札幌オリンピック (冬)
1998 　長野オリンピック (冬)

オリンピックのしゅもく

夏のオリンピック
冬のオリンピック

日本の 1998 年の冬季オリンピックのばしょ

長野けん
いど：36 38'45"
けいど：138 11'47"
人口：360 000 人
長野は東京の北西にあります。
長野の町のまわりには山がたくさんあります。

冬 (12 月・2 月) の気温はれい下で、
ウインター・スポーツにはとてもいいです。

北京
Beijing
中国
China
しゅもく
event
冬季
winter season
ばしょ
place
いど
latitude
けいど
longitude
人口
population
まわり
around
れい下
below zero
生年月日
date of birth
しんちょう
height
けいれき
career
background
11 い
11th
金メダル
gold medal
どうメダル
bronze medal

---

www.J-Olympic.com

さとや　たえ

しゅもく：フリースタイル・スキー
生年月日：1976 年 6 月 12 日
しんちょう：165 センチ
たいじゅう：55 キロ
けいれき：
1994 年リレハンメルオリンピック 11 い
1998 年長野オリンピック金メダル

---

www.J-Olympic.com

おかざき　ともみ

しゅもく：スピード・スケート (500 メートル)
生年月日：1971 年 9 月 7 日
しんちょう：163 センチ
たいじゅう：58 キロ
けいれき：
1994 年リレハンメルオリンピック
1996 年 World Single Distance Speed
　　　 Skating Championships
　　　　 どうメダル
1998 年長野オリンピック

---

www.J-Olympic

あんどう　みき

しゅもく：フィギュア・スケート
生年月日：1987 年 12 月 18 日
しんちょう：161 センチ
たいじゅう：49 キロ
けいれき：8 さいからフィギュアス
ケートはじめました。小学 5 年生で
トリプルジャンプをするこができま
した。

11

アルバイト

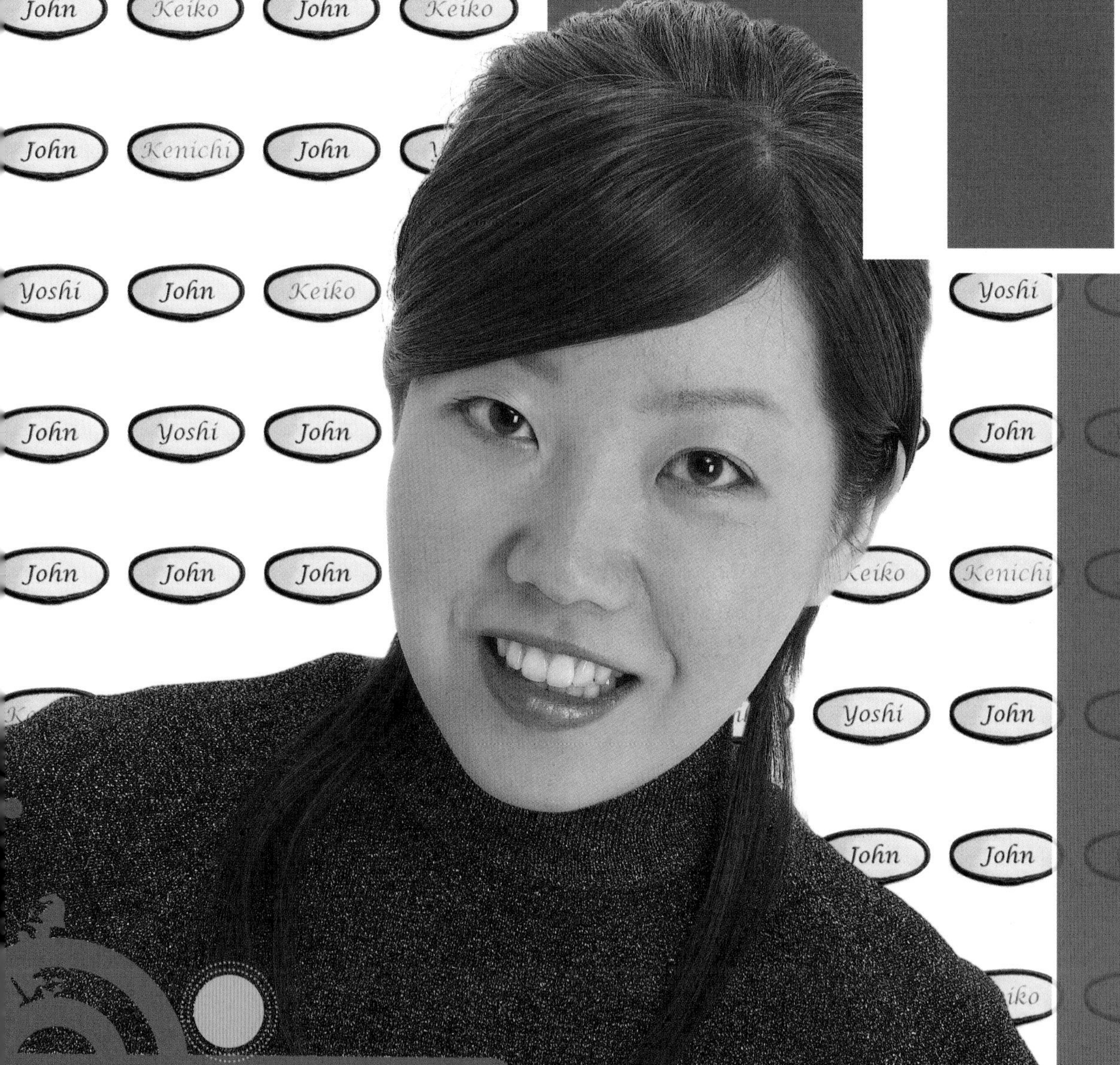

In this unit, you will learn to:

talk about things you do in non-sequential order

say what you want to become

compare two things and give your opinion

read and write a modified curriculum vitae in Japanese

prepare for a job interview in Japanese

participate in a job interview

read and write a job application letter in Japanese

recognise and write the kanji characters: 語,英,家,友,会,社,間,町

In this unit, you will learn about:

Japanese curriculum vitae

counting years according to the Japanese system

working in Japan and jobs using Japanese

more particles and their uses

John is looking for a holiday job. He has found a job advertisement in a Japanese newspaper.

アルバイト

英語のかていきょうし

中学一年生のむすめに英語をおしえてください。むすめは
一年前にオーストラリアに来ました。英語がまだ上手じゃ
ないですから、かいわやぶんぽうやさくぶんをおしえてくだ
さい。日本語がすこしはなせてあかるいせいかくの人がい
いです。でんわしてください。

西村(むら)

でんわばんごう: 8993 2459　携帯電話(けいたいでんわ): 0909 133 256

Eメール: nishimura.k@hitmail.com

home tutor
daughter
(not) yet
conversation/
　grammar/essay
person with
　a cheerful
　personality
mobile phone

John: こんにちは、ジョンです。どうぞよろしく。

Nishimura: ジョンさんですか。どうぞよろしく。ええと、ジョンさんは何さいですか。

J: 私は十六さいです。高校一年生です。

N: ジョンさん、日本語が上手ですね。あのう、ジョンさんは何年間日本語をべんきょうしていますか。

J: 中学一年生の時から、四年間日本語をべんきょうしています。それから、きょ年の夏休みに四週間日本に行ってホームステイをしました。

N: へえ、そうですか。ジョンさんはひまな時に何をしますか。

J: ええと、私はスポーツが好きですから、よく週まつに友だちとテニスをしたり、バスケットボールをしたりします。

N: ジョンさんの好きなかもくは何ですか。

J: 私の好きなかもくは日本語です。日本に日本人の友だちがいますから、日本語でEメールを書いたり、でんわをしたりします。それから、英語やれきしが好きです。よく日本のれきしの本をよみます。

N: そうですか。ええと、ジョンさんはしょうらい何をしたいですか。

J: しょうらい、会社ではたらきたいです。ぼうえき会社ではたらいて、いっしょうけんめいべんきょうして、会社の社ちょうになりたいです。

I want to work.
import/export
　company
with all one's might

11

N: へえ、社ちょうですか。すごいですね。

ええと、ジョンさんはどこに住んでいますか。

J: 町のちかくに住んでいます。

N: そうですか、じゃあ、この家までどのぐらいかかりますか。

J: ええと、三十分ぐらいです。すぐ来られますよ。

N: ああ、それはいいですね。じゃあ、ジョンさん、何かしつもんがありますか。

J: はい、ええと、時きゅうはいくらですか。

N: ええと、三十ドルですが、いいですか。

J: はい、わかりました。何曜日ですか。

N: 火曜日と木曜日とでは、どちらのほうがいいですか。

J: ええと、そうですね。木曜日はテニスのれんしゅうがありますから、火曜日のほうがいいです。

N: はい、わかりました。いいですよ。じゃ、ジョンさん、来週から来られますか。

J: はい、来られます。

N: じゃ、来週の火曜日の四時半に来てください。

J: わかりました。来週の火曜日の四時半ですね。

N: はい、よろしくおねがいします。

J: よろしくおねがいします。じゃ、しつれいします。

hourly rate

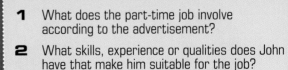

Questions

1 What does the part-time job involve according to the advertisement?

2 What skills, experience or qualities does John have that make him suitable for the job?

3 What further details about the job does he learn from the interview?

11

れんしゅう

01 Talking about things you do in a non-sequential order

一　ひる休みに何をしますか。
　　ひる休みにべんきょうしたり、友だちとはなしたり、
　　スポーツをしたりします。

二　週まつに何をしたいですか。
　　しゅうまつにえいがを見たり、
　　パーティーに行ったりしたいです。

三　夏休みに何をしましたか。
　　夏休みに友だちどうみに行ったり、
　　買いものをしたりしました。

練習
れんしゅう

02 Asking and saying what you want to become

一　ひろしくんは何になりたいですか。
　　ぼくは、いしゃになりたいです。

二　みちこさんはしょうらい何になりたいですか。
　　ええと、わたしは、びようしになりたいです。

三　まどかさんはしょうらい何になりたいですか。
　　しょうらい、きかいこうになりたいです。

03 Comparing two things and giving your opinion

一　冬と夏とでは、どちらのほうが好きですか。
　　冬より夏のほうが好きです。

二　カタカナとかんじとでは、どちらのほうが
　　むずかしいですか。
　　かんじのほうがむずかしいです。

三　ウエイターとひしょとでは、どちらのほうが
　　たいへんですか。
　　ウエイターのほうがたいへんです。

11

百三十五

漢字
かんじ

These are the kanji and their readings introduced in this unit.

ゴ | word/language

`丶 亠 亍 言 言 言 訂 訪 語 語 語 語`

I can speak five languages.

フランス語 → フランスご → French
ドイツ語 → ドイツご → German
語学 → ごがく → language study
日本語がはなせます。 → にほんごがはなせます。→ I can speak Japanese.

エイ | England/wise

`一 十 艹 艹 苎 苎 萊 英`

An English farmer with a top hat standing in front of the farm fence.

英語 → えいご → English
英語の本 → えいごのほん → English book
英語ではなします。 → えいごではなします。 → I speak in English.
好きなかもくは英語です。 → すきなかもくはえいごです。 → My favourite subject is English.

いえ／うち／カ | house/home

`丶 宀 宀 宀 宁 宕 宕 家 家 家`

A little pig in a house. 'I will huff and puff and blow your house down.'

家の中 → いえのなか → inside the house
家のちかくにうみがあります。 → いえ／うちのちかくにうみがあります。 → There is a beach near my house.
家ていか → かていか → home economics
家ぞく → かぞく → family

とも／ユウ | friend/friendship

`一 ナ 方 友`

An odd couple – one tall and one short.

友だち → ともだち → friend
友だちの家ぞく → ともだちのかぞく → friend's family
友人 → ゆうじん → friend
友好 → ゆうこう → friendship

11

百三十六

136

These are the kanji and their readings introduced in this unit.

 **あ(います)／カイ** **to meet**

Meet me at the restaurant.

ノ 入 ム 公 会 会

友だちに会います。 → ともだちにあいます。 → I will meet my friend.
五時に会いましょう。 → ごじにあいましょう。 → Let's meet at 5 o'clock.
会話 → かいわ → conversation
会ぎ → かいぎ → meeting/conference

シャ **society**

A society is made
up of men and women.

丶 ラ オ ネ ネ 社 社

社会 → しゃかい → society
会社 → かいしゃ → company
じん社 → じんじゃ → shrine
社会学 → しゃかいがく → sociology

あいだ／カン **between/duration**

Sun is shining in between
the loud speakers.

｜ 冂 冋 冐 冏 門 門 門
門 間 間 間

ひる休みの間 → ひるやすみのあいだ → during lunchtime
あさごはんとひるごはんの間 → あさごはんとひるごはんのあいだ → between breakfast and lunch
時間 → じかん → time
三日間 → みっかかん → for three days

まち **town**

An apartment block
near a T-intersection.

｜ 冂 冂 冊 田 田 町

町の中心 → まちのちゅうしん → town centre
一ばん大きい町 → いちばんおおきいまち → the biggest town
私の町 → わたしのまち → my town
みなと町 → みなとまち → port town

ぶんぽう

Talking about things you do in a non-sequential order

本を　よんだり、べんきょうしたり　します。
Sometimes I read books and sometimes I study.

ひる休みに　ジョンさんは　何を　しますか。
What does John do at lunchtime?

ひる休みに　ジョンさんは　友だちと
はなしたり、ピンポンを　したり　します。
At lunchtime John sometimes talks with his friends and sometimes he plays ping pong.

こどもの　時は　スケートボードに　のったり、
ローラーブレードを　したり　しました。
When I was a child, I sometimes went skateboarding and sometimes rollerblading.

夏休みに　買いものを　したり、レストランで
ばんごはんを　食べたり　したいです。
During the summer holidays, I want to do things like go shopping and have dinner at restaurants.

Asking and saying what you want to become

パイロットに　なりたいです。
I want to become a pilot.

有名な　かしゅに　なりたいです。
I want to become a famous singer.

しょうらい、何に　なりたいですか。
What do you want to be in the future?

しょうらい、カメラマンに　なりたいです。
I want to become a cameraman in the future.

> ! The combination of なる (to become) and たいです (to want) is 〜に　なりたいです (I want to become ...). This pattern can also be used when you ask someone what they want to be. Note: particle に is used to show what you want to become. たい acts like an い adjective, so to change the tense use い adjective rules.

> ! **I sometimes ... and sometimes ...**
> 〜たり、〜たりします is used when you want to describe some of the different actions you do, or someone else does, in a particular situation. Using 〜たり with verbs is similar to the use of や with nouns. Note: in this pattern, the same person does both activities.

文法
ぶんぽう

Which is better? A is better (than B)

すう学と　日本語とでは　どちらの　ほうが
おもしろいですか。
Which is more interesting, maths or
Japanese?

（すうがくより）日本語の　ほうが　おもしろい
です。
Japanese is more interesting (than maths).

ひこうきと　しんかんせんとでは　どちらの
ほうが　べんりですか。
Which are more convenient, aeroplanes or
bullet trains?

しんかんせんの　ほうが　べんりです。
Bullet trains are more convenient.

> **!** This pattern implies there is a choice between two items. Any adjective can be used in this comparative pattern.

> **!** より means 'than' and goes after the noun, but you don't necessarily have to use it.

Asking and saying where someone works

どこで　はたらいていますか。
Where do you work?
Where are you working?

おみやげやで　はたらいています。
I am working at a souvenir shop.

Asking and saying where you want to work

どこで　はたらきたいですか。
Where do you want to work?

きっさてんで　はたらきたいです。
I want to work at a cafe.

単語
たんご

Occupations

いしゃ	doctor
かいけいし	accountant
会社いん	office worker
かしゅ	singer
かていきょうし	tutor
カメラマン	photographer/camera operator
かんごふ	nurse
きかいこう	mechanic
きょうし/先生	teacher
ぎんこういん	banker
けいかん	police officer
げいじゅつか	artist
けんちくか	architect
コンピュータープログラマー	computer programmer
シェフ	chef
社ちょう	company president
じゅうい	veterinarian
しゅふ	housewife/houschusband
スポーツインストラクター	sports instructor
せいじか	politician
大学生	university student
タクシーのうんてんしゅ	taxi driver
ツアーガイド	tour guide
てんいん	shop assistant
にわし	gardener
はいしゃ	dentist
はいゆう/じょゆう	actor/actress
パイロット	pilot
はなや	florist
ひしょ	personal assistant
びようし	beautician/hairdresser
ぶちょう	company manager
べんごし	lawyer
やくざいし	pharmacist

Places

おみやげや	souvenir shop
カジノ	casino
ガソリンスタンド	petrol station
どうぶつえん	zoo
はくぶつかん	museum
ぼうえき 会社	international trading company
めんぜいてん	duty-free shop
りょこう 会社	travel agent

! Refer to Unit 9 for more places.

いんたいしています。	S/he is retired.

11

百四十

140

ぶんぽう Plus

Making the plain past form of verbs (た form)

There are two ways to remember how to make the plain past form of verbs (た form) – you can decide which way is easiest for you. Remember, the rules for Group 1, Group 2 and Group 3 verbs can be different!

Method A

Start with the polite past form (ました) and follow these steps:

Group 1 verbs

Chop off the ました, and depending on the syllable before ました, change the ending as follows:

い→った
ち→った
り→った
き→いた
ぎ→いだ
し→した
に→んだ
び→んだ
み→んだ

Example:

聞きました → 聞いた

Group 2 verbs

Chop off the ました and add た.

Example:

食べました → 食べた

Group 3 verbs (irregular)

Chop off the ました and add た.

Example:

しました → した
来ました → 来た

Note: 行きました is an exception. It becomes 行った。

Method B

Start with the て form:

Group 1 verbs

Chop off the て or で and add た or だ.

Example:
聞いて → 聞いた
よんで → よんだ

Group 2 verbs

Chop off the て and add た.

Example:
食べて → 食べた

Group 3 verbs (irregular)

Chop off the て and add た.

Example:
して → した
来て → 来た

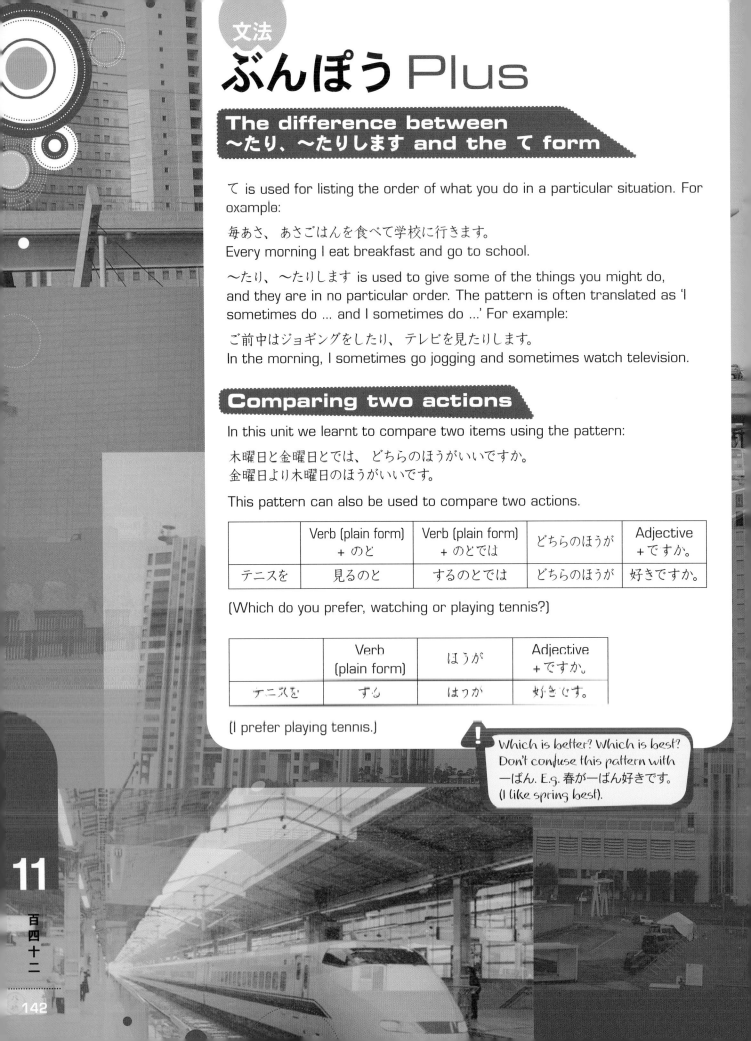

文法
ぶんぽう Plus

The difference between ～たり、～たりします and the て form

て is used for listing the order of what you do in a particular situation. For example:

毎あさ、あさごはんを食べて学校に行きます。
Every morning I eat breakfast and go to school.

～たり、～たりします is used to give some of the things you might do, and they are in no particular order. The pattern is often translated as 'I sometimes do … and I sometimes do …' For example:

ご前中はジョギングをしたり、テレビを見たりします。
In the morning, I sometimes go jogging and sometimes watch television.

Comparing two actions

In this unit we learnt to compare two items using the pattern:

木曜日と金曜日とでは、どちらのほうがいいですか。
金曜日より木曜日のほうがいいです。

This pattern can also be used to compare two actions.

	Verb (plain form) + のと	Verb (plain form) + のとでは	どちらのほうが	Adjective +ですか。
テニスを	見るのと	するのとでは	どちらのほうが	好きですか。

(Which do you prefer, watching or playing tennis?)

	Verb (plain form)	ほうが	Adjective +ですか。
テニスを	する	ほうが	好きです。

(I prefer playing tennis.)

> Which is better? Which is best?
> Don't confuse this pattern with
> 一ばん. E.g. 春が一ばん好きです。
> (I like spring best).

11

百四十二

142

A Job Interview

There are different levels of politeness in the Japanese language. As a second language learner, in a job interview the です／ます form is appropriate. Here are some ideas to consider as you prepare.

Personal details

Name:
私／ぼくは〜です。

Where/what you study:
〜で〜をべんきょうしています。

How long you've been studying:
〜年間ぐらい／〜年半、〜をべんきょうしています。

The skills/experience/qualities which make you a suitable employee:

- 〜がすこし上手になりました。
- あかるいせいかくです。
- 〜が好きです。
- 〜年前にアルバイトをしました。
- 日本語がすこしはなせます。

Finding out about the job

When:
しごとは何曜日ですか。

Hours:
何時から何時までですか。

Hourly wages:
時きゅうはいくらですか。

Starting date:
いつからできますか。

Type of job:
しごとは何ですか。

Other strategies

Opening the interview:
おはようございます／こんにちは。

はじめまして。どうぞよろしくおねがいします。

Closing the interview:
（どうも）ありがとうございました。

しつれいします。

Confirm that you have heard the information correctly (use particle ね):
木曜日の四時半ですね。

If the job requirements are not suitable, mention this politely:
（すみませんが）木曜日はちょっと…。

りれきしょ

Here is a personal history form. This is a general form that might be used if you were applying for a job in a Japanese company.

履歴書（りれきしょ）	平成十九年[1] 四月十八日げんざい		
ふりがな	ジョン・プーロス	男 ・ 女	
氏名	JOHN POULOS	いん[2] ロプス1	
生年月日（せいねんがっぴ）[3] 昭和（しょうわ）/ 平成（へいせい）	3 年 9 月 15 日 （16さい）		
本籍（ほんせき）[4]	オーストラリア		
ふりがな	37　スコット　ストリート　エッセンドン、ビクトリアしゅう、オーストラリア、〒3040		
じゅうしょ	37 Scott Street, Essendon, Victoria, Australia 3040		
電話番号（でんわばんごう）	(03) 9331 2015		

学歴（がくれき）[5]

年	月	
平成（へいせい）9	2	アベフェルディ小学校　入学
平成（へいせい）14	12	同校（どうこう）　そつぎょう
平成（へいせい）15	1	バックリー・パーク高校　入学
好きなかもく		日本語、れきし、たいいく

職歴（しょくれき）[6]

年	月	
平成（へいせい）17	5	せん車のアルバイト
けんこうじょうたい[7]		ぜんそく
しゅみ		スポーツ、読書（どくしょ）、えいが
しぼうのどうき[8]		日本語をつかってしごとをしたいからです。
本人希望記入欄（ほんにんきぼうきにゅうらん）[9]		週まつきぼう

つうきん時間[10] やく 30 分	扶養家族（ふようかぞく）[11] 0人	配偶者（はいぐうしゃ）[12] 有 ・ 無（む）

1 平成 十 九 年（へいせいじゅうきゅうねん）
In Japan, the years are often written according to the Emperor's reign. For example, the Heisei reign began in 1989 so that year is written as Heisei 1. Therefore, this application is dated 2007.

2 name stamp
3 date of birth
4 place of residency
5 school history
6 work history
7 medical conditions (serious conditions only)
8 reason for applying
9 special requests for the position
10 commuting time
11 number of dependents
12 Do you have a spouse?

12

メディア

In this unit, you will learn to:

ask and say what someone will try doing

ask and say what someone is doing while doing something else

ask and say what you have or have not done

recognise and use the plain negative form of present and past tense verbs

recognise casual speech

recognise some ending particles

recognise and write the kanji characters: 新, 読, 電, 車, 外, 国, 話, 々

In this unit, you will learn about:

Japanese manga and anime

Japanese television

more Japanese onomatopoeia

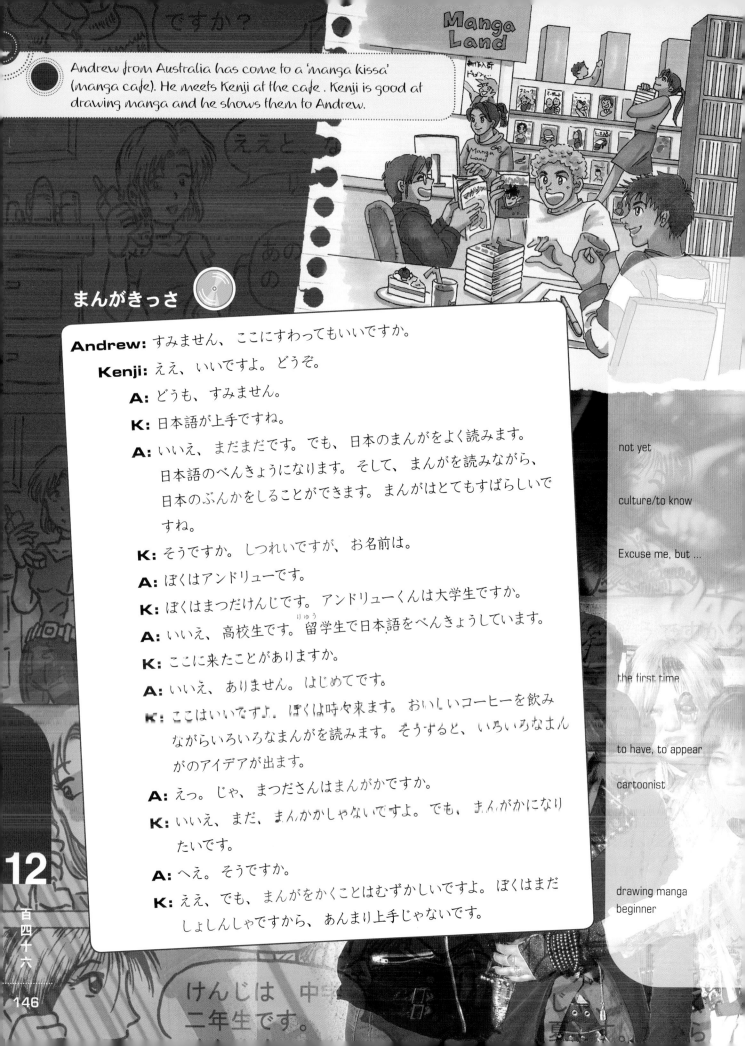

Andrew from Australia has come to a 'manga kissa' (manga café). He meets Kenji at the café. Kenji is good at drawing manga and he shows them to Andrew.

まんがきっさ

Andrew: すみません、ここにすわってもいいですか。

Kenji: ええ、いいですよ。どうぞ。

A: どうも、すみません。

K: 日本語が上手ですね。

A: いいえ、まだまだです。でも、日本のまんがをよく読みます。日本語のべんきょうになります。そして、まんがを読みながら、日本のぶんかをしることができます。まんがはとてもすばらしいですね。

K: そうですか。しつれいですが、お名前は。

A: ぼくはアンドリューです。

K: ぼくはまつだけんじです。アンドリューくんは大学生ですか。

A: いいえ、高校生です。留学生(りゅう)で日本語をべんきょうしています。

K: ここに来たことがありますか。

A: いいえ、ありません。はじめてです。

K: ここはいいですよ。ぼくは時々来ます。おいしいコーヒーを飲みながらいろいろなまんがを読みます。そうすると、いろいろなまんがのアイデアが出ます。

A: えっ。じゃ、まつださんはまんがかですか。

K: いいえ、まだ、まんがかじゃないですよ。でも、まんがかになりたいです。

A: へえ。そうですか。

K: ええ、でも、まんがをかくことはむずかしいですよ。ぼくはまだしょしんしゃですから、あんまり上手じゃないです。

not yet

culture/to know

Excuse me, but ...

the first time

to have, to appear

cartoonist

drawing manga
beginner

12

politics

to be popular

love stories/
science fiction
〔エスエフ〕/
4-frame comic

three months

A: そうですか。

K: はい。でも、日本のまんがはすばらしいです。まんがでれきしやせいじについてべんきょうすることもできます。日本ではまんがはこどもから大人（おとな）まで人気（にんき）があります。

A: そうですね。大人もまんがをよく読みますね。まつださんはどんなまんがをかきますか。

K: ぼくはれんあいやＳＦのまんがをかきます。四こままんがもかきますよ。

A: へえ、すごいですね。一つのまんがにどのぐらい時間がかかりますか。

K: ぼくはテレビを見ながら、話をかんがえたり、おんがくを聞きながら、まんがをかいたりしますから、とても時間がかかります。一つの話に、三か月間ぐらいかかりますよ。

A: へえ、たいへんですね。

K: あ、ここに、私の一ばん新しいまんががあります。どうぞ、読んでみてください。

A: わあ、かっこいいですね。ぼくも、まんがをかいてみたいです。

Questions

1 What benefits does Andrew believe he gets from reading comics in Japanese?

2 Why does Kenji like the manga cafe?

3 What types of Japanese comics are mentioned in the conversation?

4 While writing his comics, what else does Kenji do?

12

四こままんが

モグモグ ....the sound of chewing

マンガ
かおるとしんじ

©U-suke

Comic by U-suke

シーン	silence
みらい	the future
ヒューマノイドロボット	humanoid robot
かくしていて (かくす)	to hide
ごめん。	Sorry.
シクシク	the sound of sweeping
ガバッ	the sound of a sudden movement

ワーワー	the sound of bawling
うそ	a lie
ワハハ	the sound of laughing
ばか	idiot
ゲラゲラ	a cackling laugh
バシッ	a bang

12

百四十九

149

れんしゅう 🎵

01 Saying what someone will try doing

一 日本語でアニメを見てみます。

二 一人で電車で行ってみます。

三 カラオケボックスでうたをうたってみます。

02 Saying what someone is doing while doing something else

一 何をしていますか。
ジュースを飲みながら、まんがをかいています。

二 何をしていますか。
おんがくを聞きながら、Eメールを書いています。

三 何をしていますか。
あさごはんを食べながら、新聞を読んでいます。

03 Asking and saying whether you have done something before

一 日本のバラエティーショーを見たことがありますか。
はい、あります。

二 日本語のざっしを読んだことがありますか。
いいえ、ありません。

三 日本語のインターネットサイトをつかったことがありますか。
はい、つかったことがあります。

12

百五十

練習
れんしゅう

04 Saying what you won't do in the plain form [じしょけい]

一 「読みません」のじしょけいは何ですか。
読まない。

二 「話しません」のじしょけいは何ですか。
話さない。

三 「会いません」のじしょけいは何ですか。
会わない。

四 「見ません」のじしょけいは何ですか。
見ない。

五 「来ません」のじしょけいは何ですか。
来ない。

05 Saying what you didn't do in the plain form [じしょけい]

一 「聞きませんでした」のじしょけいは何ですか。
聞かなかった。

二 「行きませんでした」のじしょけいは何ですか。
行かなかった。

三 「食べませんでした」のじしょけいは何ですか。
食べなかった。

四 「しませんでした」のじしょけいは何ですか。
しなかった。

五 「来ませんでした」のじしょけいは何ですか。
来なかった。

かんじ

These are the kanji and their readings introduced in this unit.

あたら(しい)／シン　new

新

A man is making a new workbench out of wood.

```
' 　 一 　 亠 　 ヰ 　 立 　 立 　 辛 　 辛
辛 　 新´ 　 新 　 新 　 新
```

新しいテレビ	→	あたらしいテレビ	→	new television
新聞	→	しんぶん	→	newspaper
新車	→	しんしゃ	→	new car
新年	→	しんねん	→	the new year

よ(みます)／ドク　to read

読

A teacher is reading a book.

```
、 　 二 　 亖 　 言 　 言 　 言 　 言
計 　 詁 　 訪 　 読 　 読 　 読
```

まんがを読みたいです。	→	まんがをよみたいです。	→	I want to read a comic.
読み書き	→	よみかき	→	reading and writing
読み方	→	よみかた	→	the way of writing
読書	→	どくしょ	→	reading

デン　electricity

電

Rain, heat and lightning form electricity.

```
一 　 厂 　 戸 　 币 　 雨 　 雨 　 雨 　 雨
雫 　 雫 　 霄 　 雷 　 電
```

電車	→	でんしゃ	→	train
電話をします。	→	でんわをします。	→	I will make a telephone call.
るすばん電話	→	るすばんでんわ	→	answering machine
電気	→	でんき	→	light/electricity

くるま／シャ　car

車

A go-cart with wheels and an axle.

```
一 　 厂 　 厅 　 肓 　 百 　 亘 　 車
```

新しい車	→	あたらしいくるま	→	new car
好きな車	→	すきなくるま	→	the car that I like
じてん車	→	じてんしゃ	→	bicycle
車いす	→	くるまいす	→	wheelchair

漢字
かんじ

These are the kanji and their readings introduced in this unit.

 **そと／ガイ** outside/out

  外

Taro 〔タロ〕 and Tom 〔トム〕 are playing outside.

ノ	ク	タ	夘	外			

外に行きます。→　そとにいきます。→　I will go outside.
外国人　→　がいこくじん　→　foreigner
海外　→　かいがい　→　overseas
外食します。→　がいしょくします。→　I will eat out.

くに／コク country

  国

A king surrounded by a great wall.

一	冂	冂	冃	用	国	国	国

大きい国　→　おおきいくに　→　big country
中国　→　ちゅうごく　→　China
外国語　→　がいこくご　→　foreign language
国語　→　こくご　→　national language

はな（します）／はなし／ワ to speak/a talk/story

  話

Speaking a thousand words all at once

、	二	亠	言	言	言	言	言
言	話	話	話	話			

しずかに話します。→　しずかにはなします。→　I will speak quietly.
話を聞きました。→　はなしをききました。→　I heard the story.
会話　→　かいわ　→　conversation
手話　→　しゅわ　→　sign language

---

kanji repetition sign

 々

It looks like a ditto mark.

ノ	𠂊	々					

時々　→　ときどき　→　sometimes
人々　→　ひとびと　→　people
日々　→　ひび　→　day by day
年々　→　ねんねん　→　year after year

12

Saying what you will try doing

This pattern literally means that you will do it and see what it is like, or you will try doing it.

ぼくは　日本語の　まんがを　読んで　みます。
I will try to read a Japanese comic.

まりさんは　英語で　スピーチを　して　みます。
Mari will try to give a speech in English.

食べて　みてください。
Please taste/try it.

Saying what someone is doing while doing something else

Use this pattern to describe two actions a person is doing – the main thing they are doing, while doing someting else.

わたしは　コーヒーを　飲みながら、
インターネットで　チャットを　します。
I chat on the Internet while drinking coffee.

きみこさんは　しゅくだいを　しながら、
J-pop を　聞きました。
Kimiko listened to J-pop while doing her homework.

Saying what you have or haven't done

This pattern allows us to express what we have experienced or ask someone what they have experienced.

日本の　アニメを　見たことが　ありますか。
Have you ever seen a Japanese animated cartoon?

はい、見たことが　あります。
Yes, I have (seen one).

いいえ、見たことが　ありません。
No, I've never seen one (I haven't).

> ! ながら is used to show two actions occurring simultaneously. The verb directly followed by ながら is always secondary to the action in the main clause.

12

アニメ	animation, cartoons
イーメール /E メール	e-mail
インターネット	Internet
うたばんぐみ	singing show
えいが	movie
けいじばん	bulletin board
こうこく	advertisement, publicity
コマーシャル	commercial
コメディー	comedy
ざっし	magazine
時だいげき	period drama/film
じまく	subtitles
J ポップ (J-pop)	Japanese popular music
新聞	newspaper
チャット	chat
テレビ	television
テレビきょく	television station
ドラマ	drama shows
ニュース	news
バラエティーショー	variety show
ばんぐみ	TV or radio programme
ひるメロ	soapie
ふきかえ	dubbing
ほうがく	Japanese music
ほうそう	broadcast
本	book
まんが	comics
メディア	media
メルマガ	mail magazine
ようがく	Western music
ラジオ	radio

ぶんぽう Plus

Why not try using てみます？

This is a really handy language pattern to learn, but be careful to remember the following points when using it.

- みます is used for something you or someone else will try doing to see what it is like. It is often used when trying something that may be considered a challenge, but is also used for trying to do something that you haven't done before.

- みます is written in hiragana, not kanji. It is always used with a verb and is just seen as an extension of the main verb. Patterns that are used in this way in Japanese are often not written in kanji.

- In English, the verb is often omitted when you say you are trying to do something. However, in Japanese the verb must be included. For example:

  食べてみます (I'll try (eating) it).

There are lots of ways to use this pattern because we can change the tense of みます as in the examples below:

〜てみました	I tried ...
〜てみません	I won't try ...
〜てみませんでした	I didn't try ...
〜てみてください	Please try ...
〜てみませんか	Wouldn't you like to try ...
〜てみましょう	Let's try ...
〜てみてもいいですか	May I try ...
〜てみたい	I want to try ...

Using ながら correctly

Here are some of the rules for using ながら:

- the activities should both occur simultaneously

- to change the tense of the sentence, you change the final verb. This then applies to the whole sentence. For example:

  ごはんを食べながら、まんがをかきました。
  (I drew comics while I was eating dinner.)

- this pattern can only be used to talk about the actions of one person

- the more important thing you are doing goes at the end of the sentence.

12

百五十六

ぶんぽう Plus

Have you ever ...?

The たことがあります pattern is used to talk about what you have done. Can you see how this grammar is formed?

日本に行った → ことが → あります。 (I have been to Japan.)

日本に行きました。 (I went to Japan.)

For this pattern the verb before ことがあります is always in the plain past positive form. The verb at the end of the sentence must be in the present tense (i.e. あります or ありません).

Making negatives

Do you want to write something in plain form, but don't know how to make the negative tenses of other verbs in plain form? Here are some simple steps that will help:

Group 1 verbs

Change the *u* sound to *a* and add ない .

話す → 話さない
読む → 読まない
会う → 会わない

Group 2 verbs

Drop the る and add ない .

見る → 見ない

Group 3 verbs

する → しない
来る → 来ない

> Language use is always changing. Listen to young Japanese speakers to keep up-to-date.

Final particles – boys versus girls

There are a variety of final particles in Japanese – the ones that you use depend on whether you are male or female. You will often hear females use a combination of particles to show empathy or sympathy. Here are some examples:

むずかしいわよ**ね**。 (It's really difficult.)

きれいだ**わ**。 (She's really pretty.)

あたしはしらない**わ**。 (I have no idea.)

Male speakers occasionally use the above final particles but often use more masculine sounding particles, like the ones below:

これ、うまい**な**。 (This is delicious.)

おれはそうおもわない**な**。 (I don't think that's right.)

12

百五十七

Onomatopoeia

Here are some onomatopoeia that you can use in your own manga or anime.
Listen to the CD and repeat.

1　がつがつ

2　ぐちゃぐちゃ

3　いらいらする

4　わくわくする

5　ごろごろする

6　ぶらぶらする

7　だらだらする

8　どきどきする

9　にこにこする

10　めそめそする

11　ぺらぺら話す

12　りちりち書く

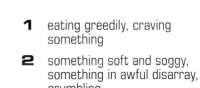

13　ぺこぺこ

14　ごちゃごちゃ

15　びしょびしょ

1　eating greedily, craving something

2　something soft and soggy, something in awful disarray, grumbling

3　to become irritated, nervous

4　to be nervous, excited, thrilled

5　to lie around, loaf about

6　to dawdle, laze around, hang around

7　to be slow at, laze around

8　to feel excited, nervous

9　to smile radiantly

10　to sob, whimper

11　to speak fluently

12　to write fluently

13　to be hungry, empty

14　a jumble, a mess

15　to be sopping wet

12

百五十八

40 HP

Insect Pokémon. Length: 3' 3", Weight: 66 lbs.

Stun Spore Flip a coin. If heads, the Defending Pokémon is now Paralyzed.

10

Leech Life Remove a number of damage counters from Venonat equal to the damage done to the Defending Pokémon (after applying Weakness and Resistance).

10

resistance

retreat cost

weakness

Lives in the shadows of tall trees where it eats insects. It is attracted by light at night.   LV. 12   #48

63/64

©1995, 96, 98 Nintendo, Creatures, GAMEFREAK. ©1999 Wizards.

Illus. Mitsuhiro Arita

メディア＆
テクノロジー

まんがかの一日

さとうかえさんはまんがかです。毎週しめきりの前、まんがかはとてもいそがしいです。先週はとくにいそがしかったです。

木曜日　ごご12.30

おきた。すぐにベッドのよこのしごとづくえで、しごとをはじめた。

1.00から

ストーリーとページレイアウトをかんがえた。

そして、えんぴつで下書きをした。むずかしかった。

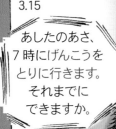

3.15

あしたのあさ、7時にげんこうをとりに行きます。それまでにできますか。

はい、がんばります。

出版社の上田さんから電話があった。

でも、できるかな

6.00

おなかがすいた。だいどころに行って、ラーメンをつくって、食べた。おいしかった。

6.30

また、しごとをはじめた。今度は下書きの上にペンでかいた。

金曜日　ごぜん2.00

ちょっとつかれた。だから、ベッドで休んだ。

6.55

あ、しまった！ねてしまった。

出版社の上田です。こんにちは。げんこうはできましたか。

じかい～

7.00

すみません！すみません！

9.30

できた！！

しめきり …………deadline	下書き ……………sketch/draft	ラーメン …………hot noodle soup
おきた……………got up	げんこう …………manuscript	今度 ………………this time
すぐに ……………immediately	とりに行きます ….go and collect	つかれた …………got tired
しごとづくえ ……work desk	がんばります ……do my best	しまった…………Oops!
はじめた …………started	出版社 ……………publishing company	ねてしまった ……fell asleep
かんがえた………thought/considered	できるかな ………I wonder if I can …	

12

百六十

160

Grammar

Here is a list of the grammar patterns introduced in Obento Supreme. The list is arranged according to the grammar patterns you can use with verbs, adjectives and nouns. Refer to pages 166 and 167 for the verb conjugation rules.

Verbs

～ます form		
Group 1	飲みます	drink
Group 2	食べます	eat
Irregular	します	do/play
	来ます	come

Do

一週間に五時間ぐらいインターネットをつかいます。

I use the Internet for about five hours a week.

Don't do

新聞をあんまり読みせん。

I don't often read newspapers.

Won't you?

いっしょにえいがを見ませんか。

Won't you come to the movies with me?

Did

メリッサさんは先週の金曜日に日本につきました。

Melissa arrived in Japan on Friday last week.

Didn't

きのう、しゅくだいをしませんでした。

I didn't do my homework yesterday.

Because

えきは家のちかくにありますから、車はありません。

I don't have a car because the station is near my house.

These patterns use the ます stem (the ます form with ます chopped off)

Go to do

こうえんにはな火を見に行きました。

I went to see the fireworks in the park.

I want to do

新しい車をうんてんしたいです。

I want to drive a new car.

While ...

私はおんがくを聞きながら、しゅくだいをします。

I do my homework while listening to music.

Potential form		
Group 1	飲めます	can drink
Group 2	食べられます	can eat
Irregular	できます	can do
	来られます	can come

Can

日本で日本人のペンパルに会えます。

In Japan I can meet my Japanese pen pal.

Gerund （～て）form		
Group 1	飲んで	drinking
Group 2	食べて	eating
Irregular	して	doing/playing
	来て	coming

Doing

今、バスていの前でかなえさんをまっています。

I'm waiting for Kanae at the station now.

Continue to do (habitual action)

三年間ぐらい日本語をべんきょうしています。

I've been studying Japanese for about three years.

Here is a list of verbs which are generally written in the て form to show a state of being or a habitual action.

しっています はたらいています

べんきょうしています 住んでいます

入っています

... and

友だちとえいがを見て、買い物に行きました。

I watched movies and went shopping with my friends.

Please do

ドアをしめてください。

Please close the door.

May I?

お父さん、車をうんてんしてもいいですか。

Dad, may I drive your car?

Mustn't

アクセサリーをつけてはだめです。

You mustn't wear jewellery.

Try doing
今ばん、インターネットでコンサートのチケットを買ってみます。
I'll try buying the concert tickets on the Internet tonight.

After ...
えきを出てから、みちをわたってください。
After leaving the station, please cross the road.

Plain (dictionary) form		
Group 1	飲む	drink
Group 2	食べる	eat
Irregular	する	do/play
	来る	come

Can do
日本語の新聞を読むことができます。
I can read a Japanese newspaper

Like/Don't like to do
まんがを読むことが好き・きらいです。
I like/don't like drawing comics.

Good at/Not good at
山中さんは人々の前で話すことが上手・下手です。
Mr Yamanaka is good at/not good at speaking in front of people.

Plain negative （〜ない） form		
Group 1	飲まない	don't drink
Group 2	食べない	don't eat
Irregular	しない	don't do/play
	来ない	don't come

I don't (casual speech)
今日、ぼくは行かない。
I won't go today.

Plain past （〜た） form		
Group 1	飲んだ	drank
Group 2	食べた	ate
Irregular	した	did do/played
	来た	came

I did (casual speech)
三時半に京都えきでまさよさんに会った。
I met Masayo at 3.30 at Kyoto Station.

I sometimes ... and sometimes
日曜日に読んだり、べんきょうしたりします。
On Sunday I sometimes read and sometimes study.

I have .../I haven't ...
まだ日本に行ったことがありません。
I haven't been to Japan yet.

日本のアニメを見たことがあります。
I have seen a Japanese animated cartoon.

Plain past negative （〜なかった） form		
Group 1	飲まなかった	didn't drink
Group 2	食べなかった	didn't eat
Irregular	しなかった	didn't do/didn't play
	来なかった	didn't come

Didn't (casual speech)
おなかがいっぱいだったから、ひるごはんを食べなかった。
I didn't eat lunch because I felt full.

Adjectives
Refer to the adjective list on page 168 and 169 for how to change adjective tenses.

い adjective	おいしい
な adjective	しずかな

And
E メールははやくて、べんりです。
E-mail is fast and convenient.

これはへんで、おかしいえいがですね。
This is a strange and funny movie, isn't it.

Doing ... is ...
かんじを書くことがたのしいです。
Writing kanji is fun.

Which is better/~er?
東京と、大阪とでは、どちらのほうが大きいですか。
Which is bigger, Tokyo or Osaka?

としょかんと、こうえんとでは、どちらのほうがしずかですか。
Which is quieter, the library or the park?

The best/~est
しんかんせんは一ばんはやい電車でした。
The bullet train was the fastest train.

一ばんすきなかもくは日本語です。
My favourite subject is Japanese.

Nouns

Places:	東京 (Tokyo)
People:	夏子 (Natsuko)
Times:	三時 (three o'clock)
Things:	つくえ (desk)
Animals:	ねこ (cat)
Activities:	買いもの (shopping)

And (joining nouns)

テーブルの上にふでばことノートがあります。

There is a pencil case and a notebook on the table.

... and ... etc.

たいいくのじゅぎょうでじゅうどうや、たいそうなどをします。

In physical education class we do judo and
gymnastics etc.

It's ... and ...

ニコルキッドマンで、ゆうめいなじょゆうです。

It's Nicole Kidman and she's a famous actress.

Which is better ... or ...?

おはしとフォークとでは、どちらのほうがいいですか。

Which is better, chopsticks or a fork?

It takes ... (time)

オーストラリアから、日本まで九時間ぐらいかかります。

It takes about nine hours from Australia to Japan.

Want to become

しょうらい、いしゃになりたいです。

In the future, I want to become a doctor.

Particle chart

か	question marker	どこから来ましたか。	Where did you come from?
が	used before		
	あります	手がみがあります。	There is a letter.
	います	ねこがいます。	There is a cat/I have a cat.
	上手・下手	えみこさんはおりがみが上手です。	Emi is good at origami.
	好き・きらい	サッカーが好きです。	I like soccer.
	can do	おはしがつかえます。	I can use chopsticks.
	but	ふるい車ですが、とてもはやいです。	It's an old car, **but** it's very fast.
	分かります	「日本語が分かりますか。」「はい、すこし分かります。」	Do you understand Japanese? Yes, I understand a little.
から	because	買いものに行きましたから、お金がありません。	I haven't got any money **because** I went shopping.
から	from	日本から来ました。	I came **from** Japan.
で	at (place of action)	家でテレビを見ます。	I watch TV **at** home.
	by (transport)	電車で行きました。	I went **by** train.
	in (using)	日本語で書きます。	I'll write it **in** Japanese.
	with everyone/by myself	みんな／一人で行きます。	Everyone will go/I will go alone.
	because	びょうきでパーティーに行けません。	I can't go to the party **because** I am sick.
	in total	ぜんぶで六人です。	There are six people **in all**.
と	and (nouns)	ケリーさんとドナさんです。	It's Kerry **and** Donna.
	with (people/animals)	友だちと出かけます。	I'm going out **with** my friends.
と〜とでは	which one?	英語とれきしとでは、どちらのほうがむずかしいですか。	Which is harder, English or history?
に	at (specific time)	三時に行きました。	I went **at** 3 o'clock.
	going to a place/direction	町に行きます。	I'm going **to** town.
	Going to a place to do an activity	山にスキーに行きます。	I am going **to** the mountains **to** ski.
		プールにおよぎに行きます。	I am going **to** the pool **to** swim
	direction of movement	左にまがってください。	Please turn left.
	for	あさごはんに何を食べますか。	What do you eat **for** breakfast?
	in	休みにうみに行きました。	I went to the beach **in** the holidays.

	in/at (location)	いぬはにわにいます。	The dog is **in** the garden.
	direction	友だちに電話します。	I'm going to telephone **[to]** my friend.
	used before		
	会います	ミック・ジャガーに会いました。	I met Mick Jagger.
	かよいます	高校にかよいます。	She attends senior high school.
	します (to decide on)	すきやきにします。	I'll have sukiyaki.
	なります	先生になりました。	He became a teacher.
	のります	ローラーコースターにのりました。	I rode on a rollercoaster.
	入ります	ピンポンのクラブに入っています。	She's in the table tennis club.
には	in/at	家にはペットがいますか。	Do you have a pet **at** your home?
ね	isn't it?/wasn't it?	それはいいですね。	That's good, **isn't it**?
の〜	of (possession)	私のケーキはどこ？	Where's **my** cake?
〜の〜に	in a position	テーブルの上にあります。	It's on the table.
		うたうのが好きです。	I like singing.
は	topic marker	私は春子です。	I'm Haruko.
は〜が	topic, subject	あねはまんがが大好きです。	My older sister loves comics.
		ベンくんは目があおいです。	Ben has blue eyes.
		私はたいいくがにがてです。	My weak point is PE.
まで	to/until	しあいは七時までです。	The game goes **until** 7 o'clock.
も	also/too	ぼくも十五さいです。	I'm **also** 15-years old.
や〜など	and, etc	ペンやノートなどがあります。	There are pens **and** notebooks **etc**.
よ	emphasis	おもしろいですよ。	It's interesting, you know!
を	object marker	ドアをあけてください。	Please open the door.
	within	日本をりょこうしたいです。	I want to travel **within** Japan.
	at	かどをまがってください。	Please turn **at** the corner.
	saying what you want	コーヒーをください。	Some coffee, please.
な	isn't it?/it is! (usually male speakers)	うまいな。	It is delicious!
よね	showing sympathy/ empathy (usually female speakers)	むずかしいよね。	It is really difficult.
わ		私はしらないわ。	I'm not sure.
		きれいだわ。	She's really pretty.

Verb chart

Here is a list of all the verbs in Obento Deluxe and Obento Supreme and an example of how to change verbs with the same ending to make the tenses you want.

Group one verbs

〜ます form	English	ます	Potential	Gerund （て）
		do/will do	can do	doing
〜います	to meet	会います	会えます	会って
〜きます	to write	書きます	書けます	書いて
〜ぎます	to swim	およぎます	およげます	およいで
〜します	to speak	話します	話せます	話して
〜ちます	to wait	まちます	まてます	まって
〜にます	to die	しにます	しねます	しんで
〜びます	to play	あそびます	あそべます	あそんで
〜みます	to read	読みます	読めます	読んで
〜ります	to sit	すわります	すわれます	すわって

あらいます to wash	行きます　to go	おします　to push	かちます　to win
うたいます to sing	*Note the て form of 行きます is	おろします to lower down	たちます　to stand
買います　to buy	行って, and the plain past is 行った.	かくします to hide	たちます　to pass (time)
かよいます to commute	かきます　to draw	けします　to switch off	もちます　to hold/carry
つかいます to use	聞きます　to listen/hear/ask	出します　to bring out/post	
もらいます to receive	さきます　to bloom	ためします to attempt/try	
	つきます　to arrive	もどします to restore/turn back	
	ぬぎます　to take off		
	はきます　to wear (lower body)		
	はたらきます to work		
	ひきます　to play (stringed instruments)		
	まきます　to roll		

Group two verbs

〜ます form	English	ます	Potential	Gerund （て）
		do/will do	can do	doing
〜い sound + ます	to get up	おきます	おきられます	おきて
〜え sound + ます	to eat	食べます	食べられます	食べて

あびます to take a shower	けします to turn off	入れます to put it	かぞえます to count
います to exist	できます to be able to	おしえます to teach	かんがえます to think
おります to get off	あけます to open	おぼえます to remember	聞こえます to be audible/can hear
きます to wear (upper body)	あこがれます to be attracted to	かけます to wear/put on (glasses)	しめます to close

Irregular verbs

	English	ます	Potential	Gerund （て）
		do/will do		doing
	come	来ます	来られます	来て
	do/play	します	できます	して

あんしんします to be relieved		ごろごろします to lie around, loaf about	
あんないします to guide		自こしょうかいします	
いらいらします to become irritated, nervous			to give a self-introduction
うんてんします to drive		せつめいします to explain	
外食します to eat out		そうじします to clean	
きんちょうします to be nervous		そうだんします to consult	
けしょうします to wear make-up		だらだらします to be slow at, dawdle along	
		ちこくします to be late	

Plain present	Plain present negative	Plain past	Plain past negative
do/will do	**don't\will not do**	**did**	**did not do**
会う	会わない	会った	会わなかった
書く	書かない	書いた	書かなかった
およぐ	およがない	およいだ	およがなかった
話す	話さない	話した	話さなかった
まつ	またない	まった	またなかった
しぬ	しなない	しんだ	しななかった
あそぶ	あそばない	あそんだ	あそばなかった
読む	読まない	読んだ	読まなかった
すわる	すわらない	すわった	すわらなかった

よびます to call	かみます to chew	あります to exist	入ります to enter
	住みます to live	おわります to finish	かぶります to wear (head)
	飲みます to drink	かかります to take time	つくります to make
		がんばります to try hard	ふります to fall (rain/snow)
		さわります to touch	かえります to return
		しまります to close	のりかえます to change (transport)
		とまります to stop	しゃべります to chat
		なります to become	おどります to dance
		はじまります begins/starts	とおります to pass through
		まがります to turn	とります to take
		分かります to understand	のります to ride
		わたります to cross	ふとります to get fat
		きります to cut	まもります to protect
		しります to know	

> **There are a few Group 1 verbs that end in an い sound plus る or an れ sound plus る. It is a good idea to learn these so you don't confuse these with Group 2 verbs which all have these sounds.**

Plain present	Plain present negative	Plain past	Plain past negative
do/will do	**don't\will not do**	**did**	**did not do**
おきる	おきない	おきた	おきなかった
食べる	食べない	食べた	食べなかった

つかれます to become tired	出かけます to go out	はじめます (I) begin	見せます to show
つけます to switch on	出ます to attend/ participate	まぜます to mix	見つけます to find
つけます to wear (accessories)	ねます to sleep	見ます to see/look/ watch	わすれます to forget
つづけます to continue	のせます to put/place		

Plain present	Plain present negative	Plain past	Plain past negative
do/will do	**don't\will not do**	**did**	**did not do**
来る	来ない	来た	来なかった
する	しない	した	しなかった

電話します to telephone	めそめそします to sob, whimper	
どきどきします to feel excited, nervous	れんしゅうします to practise	
にこにこします to smile radiantly, beaming	りょこうします to travel	
ひっこしします to move house	リラックスします to relax	
ぶらぶらします to dawdle, laze around, hang around	ろくおんします to record	
べんきょうします to study	わくわくします to be nervous, excited, thrilled	
ホストします to host		

Adjective chart

Here is a complete list of the い and な adjectives introduced in Obento Deluxe and Obento Supreme.

い Adjectives

	Positive	Negative
Present	高(たか)いです。 It is expensive.	高(たか)くないです。 It is not expensive.
Past	高(たか)かったです。 It was expensive.	高(たか)くなかったです。 It was not expensive.

Before a noun: 高(たか)いきものです。
It is an expensive kimono.
And: 高くて、ふるいです。 It is expensive and old.

あおい	blue
あかい	red
あかるい	light/bright
あたたかい	warm
新(あたら)しい	new
あつい	hot/thick (from front to back)
あぶない	dangerous
いい *	good
いそがしい	busy
いっぱい	full
うすい	thin (from front to back)
うつくしい	beautiful
うるさい	noisy
うれしい	happy
おいしい	delicious
おおい	many
大(おお)きい	big/large
おかしい	funny
おそい	slow
おもい	heavy
おもしろい	interesting/fun
かっこいい	cool
かっこわるい	ugly/idiotic
かなしい	sad
かわいい	cute/pretty
きいろい	yellow
きたない	dirty
きびしい	strict

くらい	dark/gloomy
くろい	black
こわい	scary
さびしい	sad/lonely
さむい	cold (weather)
しろい	white
すくない	few
すごい	wonderful/amazing
すずしい	cool (weather)
すばらしい	wonderful/fantastic
せまい	narrow
高(たか)い	tall/expensive
たのしい	enjoyable/fun
小(ちい)さい	little/small
ちかい	near
つまらない	boring
つめたい	cold (objects)
つよい	strong
とおい	far/distant
ながい	long
ねむい	sleepy
はずかしい	embarrassing
はやい	fast/quick
ひくい	low
ひどい	awful
ひろい	wide/spacious
ふとい	thick
ふるい	old
ほそい	thin/slender/small (diameter)
まずい	(tastes) awful
まるい	round
みじかい	short
むしあつい	humid
むずかしい	difficult
めずらしい	rare/unusual
やさしい	easy/kind/gentle
安(やす)い	cheap
わかい	young
わるい	bad

Note: いい becomes よくない in the negative, よかった in the past and よくなかった in the past negative.

な Adjectives

	Positive	Negative
Present	とくべつです。 It is special.	とくべつじゃないです。 It is not special.
Past	とくべつでした。 It was special.	とくべつじゃなかった です。 It was not special.

Before a noun: とくべつなきものです。　[It is a special kimono.]
And: とくべつで、すてきです。[It is special and wonderful.]

いや（な）	unpleasant
いろいろ（な）	various
かわいそう（な）	pitiable
きらい（な）	dislike
きれい（な）	beautiful/pretty/clean
げんき（な）	lively
ざんねん（な）	pitiful
しずか（な）	quiet
しぜん（な）	natural
しつれい（な）	impolite
上手（な）	skilful/good at
しんせつ（な）	kind
好き（な）	like
大きらい（な）	dislike a lot/hate
大じょぶ（な）	all right
大好き（な）	like a lot/love
大せつ（な）	important
大へん（な）	terrible/difficult
すてき（な）	wonderful
でんとうてき（な）	traditional
とくい（な）	skilful
とくべつな	special
にがて（な）	not good at
にぎやか（な）	lively/crowded
のんき（な）	easy-going
ばか（な）	silly
ひま（な）	free
下手（な）	unskilful/no good at
へん（な）	strange
べんり（な）	convenient
まじめ（な）	serious
ゆうめい（な）	famous
らんぼう（な）	rough/violent
りっぱ（な）	great/large/fine

かな rules

てんてん and まる

The rules for the five sound changes in ひらがな and かたかな are the same.

K sounds change to G
S sounds change to Z
T sounds change to D
H sounds change to B or P

K	か	き	く	け	こ	カ	キ	ク	ケ	コ
G	が	ぎ	ぐ	げ	ご	ガ	ギ	グ	ゲ	ゴ
S	さ	し	す	せ	そ	サ	シ	ス	セ	ソ
Z	ざ	じ	ず	ぜ	ぞ	ザ	ジ	ズ	ゼ	ゾ
	じ and ジ sound like ji not zi									
T	た	ち	つ	て	と	タ	チ	ツ	テ	ト
D	だ	ぢ	づ	で	ど	ダ	ヂ	ヅ	デ	ド
H	は	ひ	ふ	へ	ほ	ハ	ヒ	フ	ヘ	ホ
B	ば	び	ぶ	べ	ぼ	バ	ビ	ブ	ベ	ボ
P	ぱ	ぴ	ぷ	ぺ	ぽ	パ	ピ	プ	ペ	ポ

Sound combinations

If two かな are the same size (e.g. き and よ), they are said as two separate sounds. If や, ゆ, or よ are small, then two sounds run together (e.g. きょ). The table below shows the sound combinations.

や	ゆ	よ	ヤ	ユ	ヨ
きゃ	きゅ	きょ	キャ	キュ	キョ
しゃ	しゅ	しょ	シャ	シュ	ショ
ちゃ	ちゅ	ちょ	チャ	チュ	チョ
にゃ	にゅ	にょ	ニャ	ニュ	ニョ
ひゃ	ひゅ	ひょ	ヒャ	ヒュ	ヒョ
みゃ	みゅ	みょ	ミャ	ミュ	ミョ
りゃ	りゅ	りょ	リャ	リュ	リョ

Small つ／ツ

Often you see a word with small つ or ツ. For example, when you listen to the pronunciation of がっこう or ペット, you cannot hear the sound of small つ／ツ. However, there is a pause between the two sounds.

Listen carefully to the pause indicating the small つ／ツ in the following words and repeat.

がっこう	ちょっと	じゅっぷん
ペット	レッスン	サッカー

Long vowels

A long vowel in ひらがな is written as two sounds. Listen and repeat.

おかあさん	おじいさん	すうがく
おねえさん	おとうさん	

However, in カタカナ the double vowel is written as a line (ー) either horizontally as in コーラ, or vertically as in コ
ー
ラ.

クイズ タイム！

First, listen to the pairs of words and repeat. Next, listen to one of each pair, with a partner, predict which word will be said. The person who predicts correctly gets a point.

1　おかし　　　おかしい
2　きて　　　　きって
3　すてき　　　ステーキ
4　おばさん　　おばあさん
5　おじいさん　おじさん
6　きて　　　　きいて
7　しゅじん　　しゅうじん
8　して　　　　しって
9　とり　　　　とおり
10　びょういん　びよういん
11　すうじ　　　しゅうじ
12　くさい　　　きゅうさい

Special カタカナ sounds

カタカナ is used for foreign words. Yet, there are some sound combinations which cannot be written using ヤ, ユ or ヨ. Instead ア, イ, エ or オ are used. Look at these common examples:

1　[ティ]　パーティー　　　　party
2　[ディ]　ディズニーランド　Disneyland
3　[ウィ]　ウィリアム　　　　William
4　[ウェ]　ウェリントン　　　Wellington
5　[ウォ]　ウォークマン　　　walkman
6　[ファ]　ファッション　　　fashion
7　[フィ]　サーフィン　　　　surfing
8　[フォ]　フォーク　　　　　fork
9　[ジェ]　ジェット　　　　　jet

Using げんこうようし

The three rules for well-balanced writing are:

1 correct strokes
2 correct stroke order
3 correct placement for each stroke allowing the correct space between characters.

When Japanese students practise writing characters or draft a written piece such as an essay or a magazine article, they use squared writing paper called げんこうようし (see below). The squares help in the:

1 writing of balanced and even-sized characters
2 accurate positioning of characters which allows for correcting and adding ふりがな to difficult kanji.

Traditionally, Japanese was written vertically. To do this using げんこうようし , turn the paper around so that you start at the top right-hand corner and write down the column and then continue to the next left-hand column.

Today, Japanese is written vertically or horizontally on げんこうようし . To write horizontally, you start from the top left-hand corner, like in English, and write across the page. Study both styles on the next page. What differences can you find?

げんこうようし rules

Looking at the examples, on the opposite page, there are similarities and differences in the two written styles. Some of the rules for using げんこうようし are slightly different.

General rules

1 Leave three blank squares for the title.
2 Leave a blank square at the start of a new line for each paragraph.
3 No spacing between words. (Words can run onto the next line.)
4 Commas (、), full stops (。), and quotation marks (「 」) have their own square. However, when a full stop is used with a closing quotation mark, they are written together in the same square.

If (、), (。) or (「 」) are at the end of a line, they are written in the last square with the final character.

よこがき

Rules for よこがき (horizontal writing)

1 〔、 〕 and 〔。〕 or small や, ゆ, よ and つ are written in the bottom left-hand corner of the square.

2 The katakana long sound dash is written horizontally.

3 Opening quotation marks are written in the top right-hand corner and closing marks are written in the bottom left-hand corner of the square.

4 Use V between characters to insert a missing character.

5 ふりがな is written above the kanji.

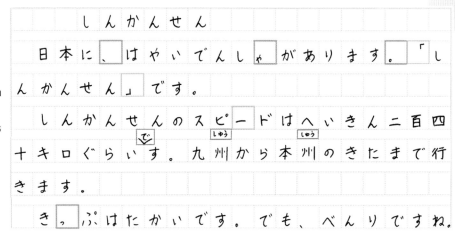

Rules for たてがき (vertical writing)

1 〔、 〕 and 〔。〕 or small や, ゆ, よ and つ are written in the top right-hand corner of the square.

2 The katakana long sound dash is written vertically.

3 Opening quotation marks are written in the bottom right-hand corner and closing marks are written in the top left-hand corner of the square. Also note their shape.

4 Use 〈 between characters to insert a missing character.

5 ふりがな is written to the right of the kanji.

Vocabulary list

日本語—英語

あ

ああ、そうですか。	Oh, really is that so? (Often used when disagreeing.)
あいだ、間	duration, between
あいたいです、会いたいです。	I want to meet you.
アイデア	idea
あいます、会います	to meet
あえるのをたのしみにしています	looking forward to seeing
あお (い)	blue
あか (い)	red
あがります	to go up
あかるい	bright
あかるい　せいかく　の人	a person with a cheerful personality
あき、秋	autumn
あきまつり、秋まつり	autumn festival
アクセサリー	accessory/jewellery
あけまして　おめでとう	Happy New Year!
あけます	to open
あご	chin
あこがれます	to be attracted by
あし	leg/foot
あしくび	ankle
あした	tomorrow
あそこ	over there (away from both the speaker and listener)
あそびに　きてください。あそびに　来てください。	Please come and play.
あそびに　きませんか。あそびに　来ませんか。	Won't you come and play.
あそびます	to play
あたし	I/me (colloquial)
あたたかい	warm
あたま	head
あたらしい、新しい	new
あつい	hot
あとで	later/after
アドレス	address
アナウンサー	announcer
あなた	you
あに	older brother (humble term)
アニメ	animation, cartoons
あね	older sister (humble term)
あの	that
アパート	apartment
あびます	to take (a shower)
あぶない	dangerous
アボカド	avocado
あまり	not really, not very often, not well

あめ	rain
あら、そう？	Oh, really?
あらいます	to wash
あらし	storm
あります	to have, to be, there is … (for inanimate objects)
あるいて	on foot
アルバイト	part-time job
あれ	that one
あれー。	What?
あんまり	not really, not very often, not well

い

い	place (e.g. The 11th place)
いい	good
いいます、言います	to say
イーメール、E メール	e-mail
いえ、家	house, home
いきます、行きます	to go
いくら	How much?
いしゃ	doctor
いす	chair
いそがしい	busy
いただきます	Let's eat. I accept the meal/drink (before eating).
イタリアご、イタリア語	Italian langauge
いちにちめ、1日目、一日目	the first day
いちばん、一ばん	number one, the most …
いっかい、一かい	ground floor
いつから	from when
いっしゅうかんにいっかい、一週間に一かい	once a week
いっしょうけんめい	with all one's might
いっしょに	together
いつつ、五つ	five
いってきます。	I'll be back (said when leaving home).
いつでも	anytime
いってらっしゃい。	Farewell, take care (said to someone when going out).
いつも	always
いど	latitude
いとこ	cousin
いま	living room
いま、今	now
いまから、今から	from now
います	to be, to have, there is … (for animals and people)
いもうと	younger sister (humble term)
いもうとさん	younger sister (someone else's)
いや (な)	awful
イヤリング	earrings
いらいらする	to become irritated, nervous
いらっしゃいませ	Welcome/May I help you?

いりぐち、入り口	entrance
いります	to need
いれます、入れます	to put in
いろ	colours
いろいろ（な）	various
いんさつします	to print
インストラクター	instructor
インターネット	Internet
インターネットサイト	Internet site
いんたいしています。	S/he is retired.
インタビュー	interview

う

うえ、上	on, above
ウエイトレス	waitress
うごかしかた	way of moving
うしろ、後ろ	behind
うそ	a lie, fib
うた	song
うたいます	to sing
うたばんぐみ	singing show
うち、家	house/home
うちわ	fans
うつくしい	beautiful
うで	arm
うどん	udon noodles
うまい	delicious
うみ	sea
うめだ　こうえん	Umeda Park
うるさい	noisy
うれしい	happy
うん。	Yes. (casual)
うんてんします	to drive
うんどうかい	sports day

え

え	picture
えいが	movie
えいかいわ、英会話	English conversation
えいがかん	cinema, movie theatre
えいご、英語	English language
えいごコミュニケーション	English communication
えー。	Really?
えーと・ええと	umm
えき	station
エスエフ（SF）	science fiction
えん、円	yen
えんぴつ	pencil

お

おいくつですか。	How old are you?
おいしい	delicious
おおきい、大きい	big, large

おかあさん、お母さん	mother (someone else's)
おかえりなさい。	Welcome home.
おかし	sweets
おかしい	funny, amusing
おかしいなあ！	A puzzling question!
おからだに　きを　つけて。	
	Take care of yourself.
おきます	to get up
おげんきですか、お元気ですか。	
	How are you?
おしえています	I am (You are) teaching.
おしえます	to teach/tell
おします	to push
おしょうがつ、おしょう月	New Year
おしり	bottom
おじ	uncle (humble term)
おじいさん	grandfather
おにさん	uncle (someone else's)
おせちりょうり	New Year's food
おちゃわん	tea cup/bowl
おつきみ、お月見	moon viewing
おつり	change
おてあらい、お手あらい	toilet
おてら	Buddhist temple
おでこ	forehead
おとうさん、お父さん	father (someone else's)
おとうと	younger brother (humble term)
おとうとさん	younger brother (someone else's)
おとこのこ、男の子	boy
おとこのひと、男の人	man
おとな、大人	adult
おどります	to dance
おなか	tummy, stomach
おなかが　いっぱいです。	I am full.
おなかが　すきました。	I am hungry.
おなかが　ペコペコ。	I am hungry. (casual)
おにいさん	older brother (someone else's)
おにぎり	rice cake
おねえさん	older sister (someone else's)
おはし	chopsticks
おはなみ、おはな見	flower viewing
おば	aunt (humble term)
おばあさん	grandmother
おばさん	aunt (someone else's)
おふろ	bath/bathroom
おふろにはいります	to have a bath
おふろば	bathroom
おへそ	belly button
おへんじを　たのしみに　しています。	
	I'm looking forward to your reply.
おぼえます	to remember
おまたせ　しました。	Thank you for waiting.
おまつり	festival

おみやげ	souvenir
おもいます	to think
おもしろい	interesting
おやつ	snack
およぎます	to swim
オリエンテーション	orientation
おりがみ	origami
おります	to get off
オレンジ（の）	orange
おろします	to drop
おわります	to finish
おわん	bowl
おんがく	music
おんせん	natural hot springs
おんなのこ、女の子	girl
おんなのひと、女の人	woman

か

カード	card
かい	floor
かいがい、海外	overseas
かいぎ、会ぎ	meeting
かいけいし	accountant
がいこく、外国	overseas
がいこくご、外国語	foreign language
がいこくじん、外国人	foreigner
がいしょくします、外食します	
	to eat out
かいしゃ、会社	company
かいしゃいん、会社いん	company employee, office worker
かいだん	stairs
かいましょうか。買いましょうか。	Let's buy it.
かいます、買います	to buy
かいわ、会話	conversation
かえります	to go home, return
かえりますか。	Will you go home?
かお	face
かわります	to save time, to save money
かがく、か学	science
かきごおり	shaved ice treat
かきたいんです、書きたいんです。	
	I want to write.
かきます	to draw
かきます、書きます	to write
かくします	to hide
がくれき、学れき	school history
かけています	wearing (glasses)
かけます	to wear (glasses)
かざん、火山	volcano
かしこまりました	certainly
カジノ	casino
かしゅ、か手	singer
かぜ	wind

かぜが　つよい	windy
かぞえます	to count
かぞく、家ぞく	family
ガソリンスタンド	petrol station
かた	shoulder
かちます	to win
カチンコチン	freezing up
がつがつ	eating greedily, craving something
がっき	musical instrument
かっこいい	cool, handsome
かっこわるい	not cool, not handsome
がっこう、学校	school
カップ	cup
かていか、家ていか	home economics
かていきょうし、家ていきょうし	
	home tutor
かど	corner
かどまつ	New Year's decoration
かならず	certainly
かにかまぼこ	crab fish cake
かねのおと	sounds of the big gong
かばん	bag
かぶります	to wear (hats)
かべ	wall
かみ	paper
かみ（のけ）	hair
かみなり	lightning
かみます	to chew
カメラマン	photographer/camera operator
かもがわ	Kamo River
かもく	subject
かよいます	to commute
から	from, because
カラオケボックス	karaoke box
からだ	body
からだに　いい	good for your body
カリフォルニア　ロール	California roll
カレー　うどん	curry noodle
かわ、川	river
がわ	side
かわいい	cute, pretty
かわいそう	poor, pitiful
かん、間	period of time
かんがえます	to think
かんこうきゃく	tourist
かんごふ	nurse
かんぱい。	Cheers!
がんばって！	Good luck!
がんばってください。	Please try/do your best.
がんばります。	I will try my best.

き

キーボード	keyboard
きいろ（い）	yellow
きおん	air temperature
きかいこう	mechanic
ききます、聞きます	to listen, hear
きこえます、聞こえます	to be audible
きじ	article
ぎじゅつ	design and technology
きせつ	seasons
きそく	rules
きた、北	north
きたぐち、北口	north entrance
きたない	dirty
きっさてん	coffee shop
きています	wearing (top half or general clothing)
きてください。	Please come.
きのう	yesterday
きびしい	strict
きぼう	request/desire
きます	to put on (top half or general clothing)
きます、来ます	to come
きもち	feeling
きもちが　いい	feels good
きゅうり	cucumber
きょう、今日	today
きょうがく	co-ed
きょうし	teacher
きょうしつ	classroom
きょうと、京都	Kyoto
きょねん、きょ年	last year
きよみずでら、清水寺	Kiyomizu Temple
きらい（な）	dislikable
ぎらぎら	pulsating heat from the sun
きります	to cut
きれい（な）	pretty, clean
きれいに	prettily
きをつけてください。	Please take care.
きんちょうします	to be nervous
きんぱつ（の）、金ぱつ（の）	
	blond (hair)
きんメダル、金メダル	gold medal
ぎんこう	bank
ぎんこういん	banker

く

くうこう	airport
くすりや	pharmacy
くち、口	mouth
くちびる、口びる	lips
くつ	shoes
くつした	socks
くつばこ	shoe box
くつや	shoe shop
くび	neck
くま	bear
くもり	cloudy
くらい	dark
くらい・ぐらい	about
くるまいす、車いす	wheelchair
くろ（い）	black
ぐちゃぐちゃ	something soft and soggy, in awful disarray, grumbling
クラス	class
クラスメート	classmate
クラブかつどう	club activity
クリーンアップジャパン	Clean Up Japan
グラム	gram
グループ	group

け

けいかん	police officer
けいざい	economics
けいさつかん	police officer
けいじばん	bulletin board
げいじゅつか、げいじゅつ家	
	artist
けいたいでんわ、けいたい電話	
	mobile phone
けいど	longitude
けいれき	background, career
ゲームします。	to play a game
けしき	scenery
けしゴム	eraser
けします	to turn off
けしょう	make-up
けしょうします	to wear make-up
げた	clogs
げたばこ	shoe box
ゲラゲラ	a cackling laugh
けん	counter for buildings and houses
げんかん	entrance
げんき（な）	lively
げんこう	manuscript
けんこうじょうたい	medical conditions (serious only)
けんちくか、けんちく家	architect
けんどう	kendo

こ

こ	counter for small round items
ご、語	language
こうえん	park
こうかんりゅうがくせい、こうかんりゅう学生	
	exchange student
こうこう、高校	senior high school
こうこく	advertisement, publicity
こうさてん	intersection
こうそく、校そく	school rules
こうてい、校てい	school yard
こうよう	the changing colour of autumn leaves
こうりつ	public
コート	coat
コーナー	corner, section
ゴール	goal
ごがく、語学	language study
ごかぞくに　どうぞ　よろしく。ご家ぞくに　どうぞ　よろしく。	
	Give my regards to your family.
ごがつにんぎょう、五月人ぎょう	
	Children's Day decorative dolls
こくご、国語	national language, the study of your mother tongue
こくりつこうえん、国りつこうえん	
	national park
ここ	here (near the speaker)
ごご	pm
ここのつ、九つ	nine
ごぜん、ご前	am
ごぜんちゅう、ご前中	during the morning
こたつ	Japanese heater
ごちそうさま。	I've finished eating/Thank you for the meal.
ごちゃごちゃ	a jumble, a mess
こと	matter, thing
ことし、今年	this year
ことしも　よろしく　おねがいします。今年もよろしくおねがいします。	
	be my friend this year too.
こども	child
こどものとき、子どもの時	
	when I was a child
この	this ...
この　へん	around here
ごはん	cooked rice, meal
コマーシャル	commercial, TV advertisement
こまったとき	when (you are) in trouble
ごみ	rubbish
ごみばこ	rubbish bin
コメディー	comedy
ごめんなさい。	I'm sorry.
これ	this one
ごろ	around (time)
ごろごろする	to lie around, loaf about
こわい	scary

こんげつ、今月	this month
こんこん	heavy snow
こんしゅう、今週	this week
コンテスト	contest
こんど、今ど	this time
こんばん、今ばん	tonight
コンビニ	convenience store
コンピューター	computer
コンピュータープログラマー	
	computer programmer
こんや、今や	tonight

さ

ざあざあ	heavy rain
サイクリング	cycling
サイクロン	cyclone
さいこう　きおん	highest temperature
さいしょ	first
さいてい　きおん	lowest temperature
ざいりょう	ingredients
さか	hill/slope
さきます	to bloom
さくぶん	essay
さくら	cherry blossom
さくらぜんせん、さくら前せん	
	cherry blossom line
さしばし	stabbing chopsticks
さしみ	sashimi
さつ	counter for books and magazines
ざっし	magazine
さっぽろ	Sapporo
さとう	sugar
さびしい	sad/lonely/I miss him.
さびしそうです。	seems sad
ざぶとん	cushion
さむい	cold
さむざむ	chilly, wintry
さゆう、左右	left and right
さわります	to touch
さんかげつかん、三か月間	
	period of 3 months
サングラスをかけます	to wear sunglasses
サンダル	sandals
さんねんせい、三年生	Common Zela
ざんねんでした。	It was unfortunate/It is disappointing.
ざんねんです。	It is a pity.

し

じ、時	~o'clock
しあい	match, tournament
シーン	silence
ジーンズ	jeans
シェフ	chef
しお	salt

じかん、時間	hour/time
じかんめ、～時間目	period
じかんわり、時間わり	timetable
じきゅう、時きゅう	hourly rate
じこしょうかい、自こしょうかいします	
	to give a self-introduction
しごと	work
しごとづくえ	work desk
じしょ、じ書	dictionary
しじょうかわらまち、	Shijokawaramachi
じしょけい	dictionary form
じしん	earthquake
しずか（な）	quiet
しぜん	nature
した、下	below, under
じだいげき、時だいげき	period drama/film
したがき、下書き	sketch
しつもん	question
しつれい しつれいします。	Excuse me/Goodbye (polite on phone).
しています	wearing (additional clothing)
じてんしゃ、じてん車	bicycle
しとしと	sprinkling rain
しぼうのどうき	reason for applying
じまく	subtitles
します	to do/play/to put on (additional clothing)
しまります	to close
しめい、し名	first name
しめかざり	New Year decoration
しめきり	deadline
しめます	to close
じゃあ、またね。	See you later.
しゃかい、社会	society
しゃかいがく、社会学	sociology
ジャケット	jacket
しゃしん	photo
しゃちょう、社ちょう	company president
シャツ	shirt
しゃべります	to chat
シャワーをあびます	to have a shower
じゆう	free time
しゅう、週	week
じゅうい	veterinarian
じゆうこうどう、じゆう行どう	
	free time activities
じゅうしょ，住しょ	address, place of residency
しゅうまつ、週まつ	weekend
じゅぎょう	lessons
じゅぎょうちゅう、じゅぎょう中	
	during lessons
じゅく	cram school
しゅくだい	homework
しゅっぱつ、出ぱつ	departure
しゅっぱんしゃ、出版社	publishing company

しゅふ	housewife/househusband
しゅもく、しゅ目	event
シュレック	Shrek
しゅわ、手話	sign language
じゅんびします	to prepare
しょうかい	introduction
しょうがく、小学	primary school
しょうがっこう、小学校	primary school/junior school
しょうじ	paper screen door
しょうしょうおまちください、少々おまちください。	
	Please wait a moment.
じょうず（な）、上手（な）	good at
しょうゆ	soy sauce
しょうらい、しょう来	future
しょうわ	Showa reign (used for giving dates)
ジョギングします	to jog
しょくじつき、食じつき	meals included
しょくれき	work history
じょしこう、女子校	girls' school
しょしんしゃ	beginner
しょちゅうみまい、しょ中みまい	
	mid-season greetings
しょどう、書道	calligraphy
じょゆう、女ゆう	actress
しりつ、私りつ	private
しりつがっこう、私りつ学校	
	private school
しります	to know
しりませんよ。	I don't know.
しろ（い）	white
しんかんせん	bullet train/shinkansen
しんごう	traffic lights
じんこう、人口	population
しんしつ	bedroom
じんじゃ、じん社	shrine
しんしゃ、新車	new car
しんせつ（な）	kind
しんちょう	height
しんねん　おめでとう　ございます。新年おめでとうございます。	
	Happy New Year!
しんねん、新年	new year
しんぶん、新聞	newspaper

す

す	vinegar
すいじょうスキー、水上スキー	
	waterskiing
すうがく、すう学	mathematics
スーツ	suit
スーパー	supermarket
スカート	skirt
すき（な）、好き（な）	to like, likeable (favourite)
すきなひと、好きな人	a person you like
すきました	to become empty

すぐに	immediately
スケートボード	skateboard
スコア	score
すごい	fantastic/amazing
すごいですね。	Isn't it great?
すこし	a little
すごろく	Sugoroku (a Japanese variety of parcheesi)
すずしい	cool (weather)
スタート	start
ずっと	all the way
ステーキ	steak
すてき (な)	nice, wonderful
スニーカー	sneakers
すばらしい	wonderful/amazing
スポーツインストラクター	sports instructor
ズボン	trousers, pants
SMAP・スマップ	SMAP (a Japanese popular musical group)
すみます、住みます	to live
すみません。	I'm sorry/Excuse me/Thank you.
すもう	sumo
すもうべや	sumo stable/school
すらすらかく、すらすら書く	
	to write fluently
すわります	to sit
すんでいます、住んでいます	
	I live...

せ

せいじ	politics
せいじか、せいじ家	politician
せいと、生と	student/s
せいねんがっぴ、生年月日	
	date of birth
せいふく	uniform
セーター	sweater, jumper
せが たかい	tall
せが ひくい	short
せつめいします	to explain
せなか、せ中	back
ぜひきてね。ぜひ 来てね。	
	You must come!
せまい	narrow
せんげつ、先月	last month
ぜんじつ、先日	the other day
せんしゃ、せん車	car wash
せんしゅ、せん手	athlete
せんしゅう、先週	last week
せんせい、先生	teacher
ぜんそく	asthma

そ

そうじ	clean up
そうじします	to clean
そうすると	when you do that
そうだ！	Oh, I remember something!
そうだんします	to consult
そうですか。	I think so.
ぞうり	thongs
そこ	there (near the listener)
そと、外	outside
その	that ...
そふ、そ父	grandfather (humble term)
そぼ、そ母	grandmother (humble term)
それ	that one ...
それから	after that

た

だい	counter for machinery
たいいく	physical education
たいかい、大会	competition
だいがく、大学	university
だいがくせい、大学生	university student
だいきらい (な)	dislike, hate
たいじゅう	weight
だいじょうぶ、大じょうぶ	alright, OK
たいせつ (な)	important
だいどころ	kitchen
たいふう	typhoon
たいへんです、大へんです。	
	It is hard.
タオル	towel
たかい、高い	expensive
たかすぎます、高すぎます	
	too expensive
だから	therefore
たくさん	many, much, a lot
タクシーのうんてんしゅ、タクシーのうんてん手	
	taxi driver
タクシーのりば	taxi stand
だけ	only
だします、出します	to put out
ただいま。	I'm home.
たたみ	tatami
たたみのへや	tatami room
たちます	to stand, to pass time
たとえば	for example
たなばた	Star Festival
たのしい	enjoyable
たのしみです。	I can't wait/I'm looking forward to it.
たのしみにしています。	I am looking forward to it.
たべます、食べます	to eat
たべもの、食べ物	food
たまがわ、たま川	Tama River

ためします	to try
たらたら	sweating
だらだらする	to be slow at, dawdle along
だれが	Who?
だれと	Who with?
タワー	tower
タンクトップ	tank top
だんしこう、男子校	boys' school

ち

ちいさい、小さい	small
ちかい	close
ちかく	nearby
ちかてつ、ち下てつ	subway
ちこく	late
ちこくします	to be late
ちち、父	father (humble term)
ちゃいろ（の)	brown
ちゃんこなべ	hot pot (sumo wrestlers' dish)
ちゅうい！	Attention!
ちゅうがく、中学	junior high school
ちゅうごく、中国	China
ちり	geography
ちります	to fall
チャット	chat

つ

ツアーガイド	tour guide
ついています	included/attached, (comes with a complementary gift)
つうきんじかん、つうきん時間	commuting time
つかいましょう	let's use
つかいます	to use
つかれています	to be tired
つかれます	to become tired
つぎ（の)	next
つきます	to arrive
つくえ	desk
つくります	to use
つくろう。	Let's make it!
つけています	wearing (for additional clothing)
つけます	to turn on
つけます	to wear, put on (for additional clothing)
つづけます	to continue
つなみ	tsunami/tidal wave
つまらない	boring
つめ	fingernails
つゆ	rainy season
つよい	strong
つり	fishing
つれませんでした。	I couldn't catch it.

て

て、手	hand
ティーパーティー	tea party
Tシャツ	T-shirt
DVDプレーヤー	DVD player
ていじせい、てい時せい	part-time high school
テーブル	table
でかけましょうか。出かけましょうか	
	Let's go out.
でかけます、出かけます	to go out
てがみを　ください。手紙を　ください。	
	Please send me a letter.
てがみを　どうも　ありがとう　ございました。	
	Thank you very much for your letter.
できました！	It's done!
できます	to be able to do, can do
できます	I can do
できるかな	I wonder if I can …
でぐち、出口	exit
テクノロジー	technology
てくび、手くび	wrist
でしょう	~don't you think?/It probably will …
です	is/are
てづくり、手づくり	handmade/homemade
てつだってください、手つだってください。	
	Please give me a hand.
デパート	department store
てぶくろ、手ぶくろ	gloves
てまきずし、手まきずし	handrolled sushi
でます、出ます	Go out/leave/exit
でます、出ます	to have (an idea)
でも	but, even
テレビ	television
テレビきょく	television station
てんいん	shop assistant
てんき	weather
でんき、電気	electricity/light
でんきスタンド、電気スタンド	
	lamp stand
てんきよほう	weather forecast
でんしゃ、電車	train
でんとうてきな	traditional
でんわしてね！電話してね！	
	Call me!
でんわします、電話します	
	to telephone
でんわで、電話で	on the telephone, by telephone
でんわをします、電話をします	to make a telephone call

と

と	and
ど	degree
トイレ	toilet
とう	counter for larger animals
どういたしまして。	You're welcome.
とうき、冬き	winter season
とうきょう、東京	Tokyo
どうして	Why?
どうぞ	Here it is (when passing things to someone)/Go ahead.
どうぞよろしくおねがいします。	Pleased to meet you.
どうですか。	How is it?
どうぶつえん	zoo
とうほく、東北	north-eastern district of Japan
どうメダル	bronze medal
どうもありがとうございました。	Thank you very much.
とお、十	ten
とおい	far
とおります	to pass by
ときどき、時々	sometimes
ドキドキします	to be nervous/excited
どきどきする	to feel excited, nervous
とくい（な）	skilful at/good at
どくしょ、読書	reading
とけい、時けい	clock, watch
どこで	Where?
とこのま、とこの間	alcove
としょかん、と書かん	library
としを　とっている、年を　とっている	to be old (for people and animals)
どちらが	Which one?
とても	very
とても　たのしいよ。	It will be a lot of fun.
となり	next to
どの	Which?
どの　ぐらい	How long?
とまります	to stop
ともだち、友だち	friend
ともだちのうち、友達のうち	friend's house
ドライブ	drive
ドラマ	drama shows
とりに行きます	to go and collect
とります	to take
どれ	Which one?
トレーナー	windcheater, jumper
どれが	Which one?
ドレス	dress

どんな	What kind of?
どんな　もの	What kind of things?

な

なか、中	inside
ながい	long
ながそでシャツ	long-sleeved shirt
なごや、名古屋	Nagoya
なぜ	Why?
なつ、夏	summer
なつ　やすみ、夏　やすみ	summer holiday
など	etcetera
ななつ、七つ	seven
なに・なん、何	what
なにか、何か	something
なにを、何を	What?
なま、生	raw
なまえ、名前	name
なまの　さかな、生の　さかな	raw fish
なりたい	want to become
なります	to become
なんがつなんにち、何月何日	What month, what date?
なんじ、何時	What time?
なんせい、南西	south-west
なんど、何ど	What temperature?
なんとう、南東	south-east
なんばい、何ばい	How many cups?
なんようび、何曜日	What day of the week?

に

にかい、二かい	second floor (first floor in Australia)
にがて（な）	bad at
にぎやか（な）	lively
にくや	butcher
にこにこする	to smile radiantly, beaming
ニコルキッドマン	Nicole Kidman
にしぐち、西口	west entrance
にちじ、日時	date and time
について	about
にています	looks alike
にほんご、日本語	Japanese language
にほんりょうり、日本りょうり	Japanese cuisine
ニューイヤーパーティー	New Year party
にゅうがく、入学	entering school
ニュース	news
にわ	garden
にわし	gardener
にんきがあります、人気があります	to be popular

ぬ

ぬいぐるみ	stuffed toy
ぬぎます	to take off clothing

ね

ネクタイ	tie
ネックレス	necklace
ねてしまった	fell asleep
ねます	to sleep
ねんがじょう、年がじょう	New Year's card
ねんせい、年生	year level
ねんねん、年々	year by year

の

のせます	to place
のち	after
のみます、飲みます	to drink
のみもの、飲みもの	drinks
のり	seaweed
のりかえます	to change (transport)
のります	to ride
のんき	easy-going

は

バーベキュー	barbeque
はい・ばい・ぱい	counter for liquid in cups and bowls
はい、はい。	Yes, go on.
はい。	Yes.
はいいろ（の）	grey
はいく	haiku (short poem)
はいぐうしゃ	spouse
はいしゃ	dentist
はいています	wearing (bottom half of clothing)
はいゆう	actor
はいります、入ります	to put in, to enter, to belong to
パイロット	pilot
ばか	silly
はがき	postcard
はきます	to wear/put on (bottom half of clothing)
はくぶつかん	museum
はこ	box
はし	bridge
バシッ	knock
はしります	to run
はじまります	to start (it starts)
はじめて	the first time
はじめまして。	I am pleased to meet you.
はじめます	to start (I start)
パジャマ	pyjamas
ばしょ	place
はずかしい	embarrassing
バスてい	bus stop
はたらきたいです。	I want to work.

はたらきます	to work
はっぱ	leaf, leaves
はな	flower/nose
はなし、話	story
はなします、話します	to talk
はなび、はな火	fireworks
はなみ、はな見	flower viewing
はなみツアー、はな見ツアー	
	flower-viewing tour
はなや	florist
はは、母	mother (humble term)
はやい	fast, quick
はやく	quickly
はやく　おへんじを　かいてください。	
はやく　おへんじを　書いてください。	
	Please write back soon.
バラエティーショー	variety show
ハリケーン	hurricane
はる、春	spring
はるいちばん、春一ばん	strong wind in early spring
はるかぜ、春かぜ	spring wind
バルコニー	balcony
はれ	fine weather
はれのちくもり	fine and later cloudy
はん、半	half
ばん	number
ばんぐみ	TV or radio programme
ハンサム	handsome
はんそでシャツ、半そでシャツ	
	short-sleeved shirt
はんズボン、半ズボン	shorts
バンダナ	bandana
パンツ	pants (underwear)
ハンドル	handle
パンや	bakery

ひ

ピアス	piercings, earrings
ひがし、東	east
ひがしぐち、東口	eastern entrance
ひき	counter for small animals
ひきます	to play musical instruments (stringed or keyboard)
ひげ	beard
ひこうき、ひ行き	aeroplane
ひざ	knee
ひさしぶりですね。	It's been a long time.
ひじ	elbow
びじゅつ	visual arts
びじゅつかん	art gallery
ひしょ	personal assistant
びしょびしょ	sopping wet, soaking through
ひだり、左	left
ひだりがわ、左がわ	left-hand side

ひだりて、左手	left hand
ひだりめ、左目	left eye
ひっこしをします	to move house
ひどい	awful
ひとつ、一つ	one
ひとつめ、一つ目	first
ひとびと、人々	people
ひなにんぎょう，ひな人ぎょう	
	girl's day dolls
ひび、日々	day by day
ひまですか。	Are you free?
ひまですよ。	I've got free time.
ひまな	free
びゅーびゅー	strong wind
ヒューマノイドロボット	humanoid robot
びょういん	hospital
びようし	beautician/hairdresser
ビル	building
ひるね	nap
ひるメロ	soapie
ひるやすみ、ひる休み	lunchtime/lunchbreak
ひるやすみのあいだ、ひる休みの間	
	during lunch break/lunchtime
ひろい	spacious
ピンク（の）	pink
ヒント	hint
ピンポン	ping-pong/table tennis

ふ

フィギュア・スケート	figure skating
ブーツ	boots
プール	swimming pool
ふうん。	I see. (casual)
フォーク	fork
ふきかえ	dubbing
ふたつ、二つ	two
ふたつめ、二つ目	second
ぶちょう	company manager
ふでばこ	pencil case
ふとい	fat
ふとっています	fat
ふとります	to become fat
ふとん	Japanese bed
ふぶき	blizzard
ふゆ、冬	winter
ふようかぞく、ふよう家ぞく	
	dependents
ぶらぶらする	to dawdle, laze around, hang around
フランスご、フランス語	French language
ブリズベン	Brisbane
ふります	to fall (rain/snow)
ふるい	old (for objects)
ぶるぶる	shivering

ふろば	bathroom
プロフィール	profile
ふん・ぷん、分	minute
ぶんか	culture
ぶんかさい	cultural festival
ぶんぽう	grammar

へ

へいせい	Heisei reign (used for giving dates)
へえ！	Wow! (casual)
ぺきん、北京	Beijing (Peking)
ぺこぺこ	hungry, empty
へた[な]、下手[な]	bad at
ベッド	bed
へや	room
ぺらぺらはなす、ぺらぺら話す	
	to speak fluently
へん	area, vicinity
ペン	pen
へん（な）	strange
べんきょうします	to study
べんごし	lawyer
へんじ	answer, reply
へんじかいてね！へんじ書いてね。	
	Write me a reply!
へんじはきんようびまで。へんじは金曜日まで。	
	RSVP by Friday
べんり（な）	convenient, handy

ほ

ほう	towards
ぼうえきがいしゃ、ぼうえき会社	
	international trading company
ほうがく	Japanese music
ほうかご	after school
ぼうしをかぶります	to wear a hat
ほうそうします	to broadcast
ほお	cheek
ボート	boat
ホーム	platform
ホームステイ	home stay
ホームルーム	home room
ほくせい、北西	north-west
ぼくたち	we (boys and men)
ほけん	personal development
ほし	stars
ポスター	poster
ホストシスター	host sister
ホストします	to host
ホストファミリー	host family
ホストブラザー	host brother
ほそい	skinny, thin
ぽつぽつ	light drops of rain
ホテル	hotel

ほん、本	book
ほん、ぼん、ぽん、本	counter for long items or bottles
ほんせき、本せき	place of residence
ほんだな、本だな	bookshelf
ほんとうですか？　本とうですか。	
	Really?
ほんにんきぼうきにゅうらん、本人きぼうき入らん	
	special requests for the position
ほんばこ、本ばこ	bookcase
ほんや、本や	bookshop

ま

まあまあ	so so
まい、毎	every
まい	counter for flat items
まいしゅういっかい、毎週一かい	
	once a week
まいつき、毎月	every month
まいとし、毎年	every year
まいにち、毎日	every day
まえ、前	before, in front of
まがります	to turn
まきす	sushi mat
まきます	to roll
まぐろ	tuna
まけます	to lose
まじめ	serious
まずい	awful, bad taste
マスク	mask
まぜます	to mix
まだ	not yet, still
まち、町	town, city
まちのちゅうしん、町の中しん	
	centre of town
まちます	to wait
まつげ	eyelash
まっすぐ	straight
まっすぐいきます、まっすぐ行きます	
	to go straight ahead
まっています。[まってます。]	
	I am waiting!
まってるよ。	I am waiting! (casual)
まで	until
まど	window
マナー	manners
マニキュア	manicure/nail polish
まもります	to protect
まゆげ	eyebrow
まよい　ばし	wandering chopsticks
マヨネーズ	mayonnaise
まるい	round
まわり	around
まんが	comics
まんがか、まんが家	cartoonist

まんがきっさ	manga café
まんがをかくこと	drawing manga
マンション	apartment/apartment building

み

みえます、見えます	to be visible, can see
みぎ、右	right
みぎがわ、右がわ	right-hand side
みぎて、右手	right hand
みぎめ、右目	right eye
みじかい	short
みずぎ、水ぎ	bathers, swimwear
みせ	shops
みせます、見せます	to show
みち	street, road
みつけます、見つけます	to find
みっつ、三つ	three
み・つつめ、二つ目	third
みてみましょう、見てみましょう	
	Let me just check.
みどり（の）	green
みなとまち、みなと町	port town
みなみ、南	south
みなみぐち、南口	southern entrance
みます、見ます	to see, watch, look
みみ、耳	ear
みみがとおい、耳が　とおい	
	deaf, difficulty hearing
みらい、み来	future
みんな	everyone
みんなで	by everyone

む

むかえに　いきます、むかえに行きます	
	to go and meet
むしあつい	humid
むずかしい	difficult
むすめ	daughter
むっつ、六つ	six
むらさき（の）	purple

め

め、目	eye
めいじん、名人	expert, master, professional
めがね	glasses
めがねをかけます	to wear glasses
めそめそする	to sob, whimper
メディア	media
メニュー	menu
メルマガ	mail magazine
めんぜいてん	duty-free shop

も

も	also
もういちどいってください。 もう一ど言ってください。	Please repeat it.
もうすぐ	soon
もうちょっと…	A little more ...
モグモグ	the sound of chewing
もしもし	hello (on the phone)
もちかた	way to hold
もちます	to carry, hold
もちろん	of course
もってくるもの、 もって来るもの	things to bring
もどします	to return
ものさし	ruler
もみじの　はっぱ	maple leaves
ももいろ（の）	peach-coloured
もらいました	received

や

や	and ... etc.
やおや	greengrocer
やきとり	yakitori, chicken skewers
やくざいし	pharmacist
やさかじんじゃ、 やさかじん社	Yasaka Shrine
やさしい	kind, gentle, easy
やさしそう	looks kind
やすい、 安い	cheap, less expensive
やすみ、 休み	holiday
やせている	thin, slim, skinny
やっつ、 八つ	eight
やま、 山	mountain
やまぐち、 山口	Yamaguchi (surname)
やまのぼり、 山のぼり	mountain climbing
やめます	to quit

ゆ

ゆうこう、 友好	friendship
ゆうじん、 友人	friend
ゆうびんきょく	post office
ゆうめい（な）、 ゆう名な	famous
ゆかた	cotton kimono
ゆき	snow
ゆきだるま	snowman
ゆっくり	slowly
ゆっくり言ってください。	Please speak more slowly.
ゆび	fingers
ゆびわ	ring

よ

ようがく	Western music
ようしつ	Western-style room
ようしょく、 よう食	Western food
よかった。	It was good/It is a relief/Great!
よこ	next to
よこのみち	side path/road
よせばし	pulling chopsticks
よっかかん、 4日間	four days
よっつ、 四つ	four
よにんぶん、 4人分、 四人分	for 4 people
よびます	to call
よみかき、 読み書き	reading and writing
よみかた、 読みかた	way of writing
よみせ	night-time stalls
よみます、 読みます	to read
より	from, than
よんこままんが、 四こままんが	four-frame comic

ら

ラーメン	hot noodle soup
らいげつ、 来月	next month
らいしゅう、 来週	next week
らいねん、 来年	next year
らくがき	graffiti
ラサールこうこう、 高校	La Salle High School
ラジオ	radio
ラミントン	lamington
らんぼう（な）	rough, violent

り

りきし	sumo wrestler
りっぱ（な）	great, large, fine
リボン	ribbon
りゅうがくせい、 りゅう学生	exchange student
りょうり	cooking
りょかん	Japanese-style inn
りょこう、 りょ行	travel
りょこうがいしゃ、 りょ行会社	travel agent
りょこうします、 りょ行します	to travel
リラックスします	to relax
りれきしょ、 りれき書	personal history form

る

るすばんでんわ、 るすばん電話	answering machine

れ

れいか、れい下	below zero degrees
れいど	zero degrees
れきし	history
レジ	register, cashier
レポート	report
れんあい	love story
れんしゅうします	to practise

ろ

ローラーブレード	rollerblading
ろくおんします	to record
ロックコンサート	rock concert
ロックバンド	rock band
ろてんぶろ	outdoor bath

わ

わあー。	Wow!
ワーワー	the sound of loud crying
わかい	young
わかりました。分かりました。	
	I understand. (I have understood.)
わかります、分かります	to understand
わくわく	exciting
わくわくする	to be nervous, excited, thrilled
わさび	wasabi
わしつ	tatami room (traditional style)
わしょく、わ食	Japanese food
わすれないで！	Don't forget!
わすれます	to forget
わたしたち、私たち	we
わたしの、私の	my
わたります	to cross
ワハハ	the sound of laughing
わるい	bad
ワンピース	one-piece dress

Vocabulary list
英語ー日本語
A

able to do, can do	できます
about	くらい，ぐらい
about	〜について
accessory/jewellery	アクセサリー
accountant	かいけいし
actor	はいゆう
actress	じょゆう、女ゆう
address	アドレス
address, place of residency	
	じゅうしょ、住しょ
adult	おとな、大人
advertisement, publicity	こうこく
aeroplane	ひこうき、ひ行き
after	あとで、のち
after school	ほうかご
after that	それから
air temperature	きおん
airport	くうこう
alcove	とこのま、とこの間
a little	すこし
a little more …	もうちょっと…
all the way	ずっと
alright, okay	だいじょうぶ、大じょうぶ
also	も
always	いつも
am	ごぜん、ご前
amazing	すごい、すばらしい
and	と
and … etc.	や
animation, cartoons	アニメ
ankle	あしくび
announcer	アナウンサー
answer, reply	へんじ
answering machine	るすばんでんわ、るすばん電話
anytime	いつでも
apartment	アパート
apartment (building)	マンション
appear, perform	〜にでる、〜出る
A puzzling question!	おかしいなあ！
architect	けんちくか、けんちく家
Are you free?	ひまですか。
area, vicinity	へん
arm	うで
around	まわり
around (a certain time)	ごろ
around here	この　へん
arrive	つきます
art gallery	びじゅつかん

article	きじ
artist	げいじゅつか、げいじゅつ家
asthma	ぜんそく
athlete	せんしゅ、せん手
Attention!	ちゅうい！
attracted by	あこがれます
attractive, trendy	かっこいい
audible	きこえます、聞こえます
aunt (humble term)	おば
aunt (someone else's)	おばさん
autumn	あき、秋
autumn festival	あきまつり、秋まつり
autumn tints on leaves	こうよう
avocado	アボカド
awful	いや（な）ひどい
awful, bad taste	まずい

B

back	せなか、せ中
background, career	けいれき
bad	わるい
bad at	にがて（な）
bad at	へた（な）下手（な）
bag	かばん
bakery	パンや
balcony	バルコニー
bandana	バンダナ
bank	ぎんこう
banker	ぎんこういん
barbeque	バーベキュー
bathers, swimwear	みずぎ、水ぎ
bathroom	おふろば、おふろ
bear	くま
beard	ひげ
beautician/hairdresser	
	びようし
beautiful	うつくしい
because	から
become	なります
bed	ベッド
bedroom	しんしつ
before, in front of	まえ、前
beginner	しょしんしゃ
behind	うしろ、後ろ
Beijing (Peking)	ぺきん、北京
belly button	おへそ
below, under	した、下
below zero degrees	れいか、れい下
bicycle	じてんしゃ、じてん車
big, large	おおきい、大きい
birthday	せいねんがっぴ、生年月日
black	くろい
blizzard	ふぶき

blond (hair)	きんぱつ（の）、金ぱつ（の）
bloom	さきます
blue	あおい
boat	ボート
body	からだ
book	ほん、本
bookcase	ほんばこ、本ばこ
bookshelf	ほんだな、本だな
bookshop	ほんや、本や
boots	ブーツ
boring	つまらない
bottom	おしり
bowl	おわん
box	はこ
boy	おとこのこ、男の子
boys' school	だんしこう、男子校
bridge	はし
bright	あかるい
Brisbane	ブリズベン
broadcast	ほうそうします
bronze medal	どうメダル
brown	ちゃいろ（の）
Buddhist temple	おてら
building	ビル
bullet train/shinkansen	しんかんせん
bulletin board	けいじばん
bus stop	バスてい
busy	いそがしい
but, even	でも
butcher	にくや
buy	かいます、買います
by everyone	みんなで

C

cackling laugh	ゲラゲラ
California roll	カリフォルニアロール
call	よびます
Call me!	でんわしてね！電話してね！
calligraphy	しょどう、書どう
car wash	せんしゃ、せん車
card	カード
carry, hold	もちます
cartoonist	まんがか、まんが家
casino	カジノ
centre of town	まちのちゅうしん、町の中しん
certainly	かならず
Certainly.	かしこまりました。
chair	いす
change	おつり
change (transport)	のりかえます
chat	しゃべります
chat	チャット
cheap	やすい、安い

cheek	ほお
Cheers.	かんぱい。
chef	シェフ
cherry blossom	さくら
cherry blossom line	さくらぜんせん、さくら前せん
chew	かみます
chicken skewers	やきとり
Children's Day decorative dolls	ごがつにんぎょう、五月人ぎょう
chilly, wintry	さむざむ
chin	あご
China	ちゅうごく、中国
chopsticks	おはし
cinema, movie theatre	えいがかん
class	クラス
classmate	クラスメート
classroom	きょうしつ
clean	そうじ（を）します
clean up	そうじ
clock, watch	とけい、時けい
clogs	げた
close	ちかい
close	しめます、しまります
cloudy	くもり
club activity	クラブかつどう
coat	コート
co-ed	きょうがく
coffee shop	きっさてん
cold	さむい
colours	いろ
come	きます、来ます
comedy	コメディー
comics	まんが
commercial, TV advertisement	コマーシャル
commute	かよいます
commuting time	つうきんじかん、つうきん時間
company	かいしゃ、会社
company employee, office worker	かいしゃいん、会社いん
company manager	ぶちょう
company president	しゃちょう、社ちょう
competition	たいかい、大会
computer	コンピューター
computer programmer	コンピュータープログラマー
consult	そうだんします
contest	コンテスト
continue	つづけます
convenience store	コンビニ
convenient, handy	べんり（な）
conversation	かいわ、会話
cooked rice, meal	ごはん
cooking	りょうり

cool (weather)	すずしい
cool, handsome	かっこいい
corner	かど
corner, section	コーナー
cotton kimono	ゆかた
count	かぞえます
counter for books and magazines	さつ
counter for buildings and houses	けん
counter for flat items	まい
counter for larger animals	とう
counter for long items or bottles	ほん、ぼん、ぽん、本
counter for machinery	だい
counter for small animals	ひき
counter for small round items	こ
counter of liquid in cups and bowls	はい・ばい・ぱい
cousin	いとこ
crab fish cake	かにかまぼこ
cram school	じゅく
cross	わたります
cry loudly	ワーワー
cucumber	きゅうり
cultural festival	ぶんかさい
culture	ぶんか
cup	カップ
curry noodles	カレーうどん
cushion	ざぶとん
cut	きります
cute, pretty	かわいい
cycling	サイクリング
cyclone	サイクロン

D

dance	おどります
dangerous	あぶない
dark	くらい
date and time	にちじ、日時
date of birth	せいねんがっぴ、生年月日
daughter	むすめ
dawdle, laze around	ぶらぶらする
dawdle, relax	だらだらする
day by day	ひび、日々
deaf, difficulty hearing	みみがとおい、耳が　とおい
degree	ど
delicious	おいしい、うまい
dentist	はいしゃ
department store	デパート
departure	しゅっぱつ、出ぱつ

dependents	ふようかぞく、ふよう家ぞく
design and technology	ぎじゅつ
desk	つくえ
dictionary	じしょ、じ書
dictionary form	じしょけい
difficult	むずかしい
dirty	きたない
dislikable	きらい（な）
dislike, hate	だいきらい（な）
do, play	します
doctor	いしゃ
Don't forget!	わすれないで！
drama shows	ドラマ
draw	かきます
drawing manga	まんがをかくこと
dress	ドレス、ワンピース
drink	のみます、飲みます
drinks	のみもの、飲みもの
drive	うんてんします、ドライブ
drop	おろします
dubbing	ふきかえ
duration, between	あいだ、間
during lessons	じゅぎょうちゅう、じゅぎょう中
during lunch break/lunchtime	ひるやすみのあいだ、ひる休みの間
during the morning	ごぜんちゅう、ご前中
duty free shop	めんぜいてん
DVD player	DVD プレーヤー

E

ear	みみ、耳
earrings	イヤリング
earthquake	じしん
east	ひがし、東
eastern entrance	ひがしぐち、東口
easy-going	のんき
eat	たべます、食べます
eat out	がいしょくします、外食します
eating greedily, craving something	がつがつ
eating sound for chewing	モグモグ
economics	けいざい
eight	やっつ、八つ
elbow	ひじ
electricity/light	でんき、電気
e-mail	イーメール・E メール
embarrassing	はずかしい
empty	すきました
English communication	えいごコミュニケーション
English conversation	えいかいわ、英会話
English language	えいご、英語
enjoyable	たのしい

enter	はいります、入ります
entering school	にゅうがく、入学
entrance	いりぐち、入り口、げんかん
eraser	けしゴム
essay	さくぶん
etcetera	など
event	しゅもく、しゅ目
every	まい、毎
every day	まいにち、毎日
every month	まいつき、毎月
every year	まいとし、毎年
everyone	みんな
exchange student	こうかんりゅうがくせい、こうかんりゅう学生
excited, nervous	どきどきする
exciting	わくわく
Excuse me/Goodbye.	しつれいします。
exit	でぐち、出口
expensive	たかい、高い
expert, master, professional	めいじん、名人
explain	せつめいします
eye	め、目
eyebrow	まゆげ
eyelash	まつげ

F

face	かお
fall	ちりました
fall (rain/snow)	ふります
family	かぞく、家ぞく
famous	ゆうめい（な）、ゆう名な
fans	うちわ
fantastic	すごい
far	とおい
Farewell/Take care.	いってらっしゃい。
fast, quick	はやい
fat	ふとっています、ふとい
father (humble term)	ちち、父
father (someone else's)	おとうさん、お父さん
feeling	きもち
feels good	きもちが いい
festival	おまつり
figure skating	フィギィア・スケート
find	みつけます、見つけます
fine and later cloudy	はれのちくもり
fine weather	はれ
fingernails	つめ
fingers	ゆび
finish	おわります
fireworks	はなび、はな火
first	ひとつめ、一つ目、さいしょ
first name	しめい、し名
first time	はじめて

百
九
十

190

fishing	つり
five	いつつ、五つ
floor	かい
florist	はなや
flower viewing	おはなみ、おはな見
flower-viewing tour	はなみツアー、はな見ツアー
flowers	はな
food	たべもの、食べもの
for example	たとえば
for four people	よにんぶん、4人分、四人分
forehead	おでこ
foreign language	がいこくご、外国語
foreigner	がいこくじん、外国人
forget	わすれます
fork	フォーク
four	よっつ、四つ
four days	よっかかん、4日間
four-frame comic	よんこままんが、四こままんが
free	ひま（な）
free time	じゆう
free time activities	じゆうこうどう、じゆう行どう
freezing up	カチンコチン
French language	フランスご、フランス語
friend	ともだち、友だち、ゆうじん、友人
friend's house	ともだちのうち、友達のうち
friendship	ゆうこう、友好
from	から
from now	いまから、今から
from when	いつから
from, than	より
funny	おかしい
future	しょうらい、しょう来、みらい、み来

G

garden	にわ
gardener	にわし
geography	ちり
get off	おります
get up	おきます
girl	おんなのこ、女の子
girl's day dolls	ひなにんぎょう、ひな人ぎょう
girls' school	じょしこう、女子校
Give my regards to your family.
	ごかぞくに　どうぞ　よろしく。ご家ぞくに どうぞ　よろしく。
glasses	めがね
gloves	てぶくろ、手ぶくろ
go	いきます、行きます
go and meet	むかえに　いきます、むかえに行きます
go home, return	かえります
go out	でかけます、出かけます
go out, leave, exit	でます、出ます
go straight ahead	まっすくいきます、まっすぐ行きます

goal	ゴール
gold medal	きんメダル、金メダル
good	いい
good at	じょうず（な）、上手（な）
good for your body	からだに　いい
Good luck!	がんばって！
graffiti	らくがき
gram	グラム
grammar	ぶんぽう
grandfather (humble term)
	そふ、そ父
grandmother (humble term)
	そぼ、そ母
grandfather	おじいさん
grandmother	おばあさん
great, large, fine	りっぱ（な）
green	みどり（の）
greengrocer	やおや
grey	はいいろ（の）
ground floor	いっかい、一かい
group	グループ

H

haiku (short poem)	はいく
hair	かみ（のけ）
half	はん、半
hand	て、手
handle	ハンドル
handmade/homemade	てづくり、手づくり
handrolled sushi	てまきずし、手まきずし
handsome	ハンサム（な）
happy	うれしい
Happy New Year!	あけまして　おめでとう
hat	ぼうし
have, to be, there is ... (for inanimate objects)
	あります
have a bath	おふろにはいります
have a shower	シャワーをあびます
head	あたま
heavy rain	ざあざあ
heavy snow	こんこん
height	しんちょう
Heisei reign (used for giving dates)
	へいせい
hello (on the phone)	もしもし
here (near the speaker)	ここ
Here it is. Go ahead.	どうぞ。
hide	かくします
highest temperature	さいこう　きおん
hill/slope	さか
hint	ヒント
history	れきし
holiday	やすみ、休み
home economics	かていか、家ていか

home room	ホームルーム
home stay	ホームステイ
home tutor	かていきょうし、家ていきょうし
homework	しゅくだい
hospital	びょういん
host	ホストします
host brother	ホストブラザー
host family	ホストファミリー
host sister	ホストシスター
hot	あつい
hot pot (sumo wrestlers dish)	ちゃんこなべ
hotel	ホテル
hour/time	じかん、時間
hourly rate	じきゅう、時きゅう
house, home	いえ、うち、家
housewife/househusband	しゅふ
How are you?	おげんきですか、お元気ですか。
How is it?	どうですか
How long?	どの　ぐらい
How many cups?	なんばい、何ばい
How much?	いくら
How old are you?	おいくつですか。
humanoid robot	ヒューマノイドロボット
humid	むしあつい
hungry, empty	ぺこぺこ
hurricane	ハリケーン

I

I, me (colloquial)	あたし
I am full.	おなかが　いっぱいです。
I am hungry.	おなかが　すきました。
I am hungry. (casual)	おなかが　ペコペコ。
I am looking forward to it.	たのしみにしています。
I am pleased to meet you.	はじめまして。
I am teaching.	おしえています
I am waiting!	まっています／まってます。
I am waiting! (casual)	まってるよ。
I can do	できます
I can't wait/I'm looking forward to it.	たのしみです。
I couldn't catch (it).	つれませんでした。
idea	アイデア
I don't know	しりませんよ。
I live...	すんでいます、住んでいます
I'll be back.	いってきます。
I'm home.	ただいま。
I'm looking forward to your reply.	おへんじを　たのしみに　しています。
important	たいせつ（な）
I'm sorry.	ごめんなさい。

I'm sorry/Excuse me/Thank you.	すみません。
included/attached	ついています
ingredients	ざいりょう
inside	なか、中
instructor	インストラクター
interesting, funny	おもしろい
international trading company	ぼうえきがいしゃ、ぼうえき会社
Internet	インターネット
Internet site	インターネットサイト
intersection	こうさてん
interview	インタビュー
introduction	しょうかい
irritated, nervous	いらいらする
is/are	です
I see. (casual)	ふうん。
Isn't it great?	すごいですね。
Italian langauge	イタリアご、イタリア語
I think so.	そうですか。
It is a pity.	ざんねんです。
It is hard.	たいへんです、大へんです。
It's been a long time.	ひさしぶりですね。
It's done!	できました！
It's time.	時間です。
It was good/It is a relief/Great!	よかった。
It was unfortunate/It is disappointing.	ざんねんでした。
It will be a lot of fun.	とても　たのしいよ。
I understand (I have understood).	わかりました。分かりました。
I've finished eating/Thank you for the meal.	ごちそうさま。
I've got free time.	ひまですよ。
I want to meet you.	あいたいです、会いたいです。
I want to work.	はたらきたいです。
I want to write	かきたいんです、書きたいんです。
I will try my best.	がんばります。

J

jacket	ジャケット
Japanese bed	ふとん
Japanese cuisine	にほんりょうり、日本りょうり
Japanese food	わしょく、わ食
Japanese heater	こたつ
Japanese language	にほんご、日本語
Japanese music	ほうがく
Japanese popular music	J - POP
Japanese-style inn	りょかん
jeans	ジーンズ
jewellery	アクセサリー
jog	ジョギングします

jumble, a mess	ごちゃごちゃ
junior high school	ちゅうがく、中学

K

Kamo River	かもがわ
karaoke box	カラオケボックス
kendo	けんどう
keyboard	キーボード
kind	しんせつ (な)
kind, gentle, easy	やさしい
kitchen	だいどころ
Kiyomizu Temple	きよみずでら、清水寺
knee	ひざ
knock	バシッ
know	しります
Kyoto	きょうと、京都

L

lamington	ラミントン
lamp stand	でんきスタンド、電気スタンド
language	～ご、～語
language study	ごがく、語学
La Salle High School	ラサールこうこう、高校
last month	せんげつ、先月
last week	せんしゅう、先週
last year	きょねん、きょ年
late	ちこくします
later	あとで
latitude	いど
lawyer	べんごし
leaf	はっぱ
leave, participate	～でます
left	ひだり、左
left and right	さゆう、左右
left eye	ひだりめ、左目
left hand	ひだりて、左手
left-hand side	ひだりがわ、左がわ
leg/foot	あし
lessons	じゅぎょう
Let me just check.	みてみましょう、見てみましょう
Let's buy it.	かいましょうか。買いましょうか。
Let's eat. I accept the meal/drink (before eating). いただきます。	
Let's go out.	でかけましょうか。出かけましょうか
Let's make it!	つくろう。
let's use	つかいましょう
library	としょかん、と書かん
lie, fib	うそ
lie around, loaf about	ごろごろする
light drops of rain	ぽつぽつ
lightning	かみなり
like, likeable (favourite)	すき (な)、好き (な) lips
lips	くちびる

listen, hear	ききます、聞きます
live	すみます、住みます
lively	にぎやか (な)、げんき (な)
living room	いま
long	ながい
longitude	けいど
long-sleeved shirt	ながそでシャツ
looking forward to seeing あえるのをたのしみにしています	
looks alike	にています
looks kind	やさしそう
lose	まけます
love	れんあい
lowest temperature	さいてい　きおん
lunchtime/lunchbreak	ひるやすみ、ひる休み

M

magazine	ざっし
mail magazine	メルマガ
make	つくります
make a telephone call	でんわをします、電話をします
make-up	けしょう
man	おとこのひと、男の人
manga café	まんがきっさ
manicure/nail polish	マニキュア
manners	マナー
manuscript	げんこう
many, much, a lot	たくさん
maple leaves	もみじの　はっぱ
mask	マスク
match, tournament	しあい
mathematics	すうがく、すう学
matter, thing	こと
mayonnaise	マヨネーズ
meals included	しょくじつき、食じつき
mechanic	きかいこう
media	メディア
medical conditions (serious only) けんこうじょうたい	
meet	あいます、会います
meeting	かいぎ、会ぎ
menu	メニュー
mid-season greetings	しょちゅうみまい、しょ中みまい
minute	ふん・ぶん、分
mix	まぜます
mobile phone	けいたいでんわ、けいたい電話
moon viewing	おつきみ、お月見
mother (humble term)	はは、母
mother (someone else's) おかあさん、お母さん	
mountain	やま、山
mountain climbing	やまのぼり、山のぼり
mouth	くち、口

move house	ひっこしをします	north-eastern district of Japan	
movie	えいが		とうほく、東北
museum	はくぶつかん	north entrance	きたぐち、北口
music	おんがく	north west	ほくせい、北西
musical instrument	がっき	nose	はな
my	わたしの、私の	not cool, ugly	かっこわるい

N

Nagoya	なごや、名古屋	not really, not very often, not well	
			あまり、あんまり
name	なまえ、名前	not yet, still	まだ
nap	ひるね	now	いま、今
narrow	せまい	number	ばん
national language	こくご、国語	number one, the most ...	
national park	こくりつこうえん、国りつこうえん		いちばん、一ばん
natural hot springs	おんせん	nurse	かんごふ
nature	しぜん		
navel	おへそ		

O

nearby	ちかく	o'clock	じ、時
neck	くび	of course	もちろん
necklace	ネックレス	Oh, I remember something!	
necktie	ネクタイ		そうだ!
nervous	きんちょうします	Oh, really is that so? (Often used when disagreeing.)	
nervous, excited	ドキドキします		ああ、そうですか。
nervous, excited, thrilled		Oh, really?	あら、そう?
	わくわくする	old (for objects)	ふるい
new	あたらしい、新しい	old (for people and animals)	
new car	しんしゃ、新車		としを とっている、年を とっている
New Year	おしょうがつ、おしょう月	older brother (humble term)	
new year	しんねん、新年		あに
New Year decoration	しめかざり	older brother (someone else's)	
New Year party	ニューイヤーパーティー		おにいさん
New Year's card	ねんがじょう、年がじょう	older sister (humble term)	
New Year's decoration	かじょう		あね
New Year's food	おせちりょうり	older sister (someone else's)	
news	ニュース		おねえさん
newspaper	しんぶん、新聞	on foot	あるいて
next	つぎ (の)	on the telephone, by telephone	
next month	らいげつ、来月		でんわで、電話で
next to	となり、よこ	on, above	うえ、上
next week	らいしゅう、来週	once a week	いっしゅうかんにいっかい、一週間に一かい、まいしゅういっかい、毎週一かい
next year	らいねん、来年	one	ひとつ、一つ
nice, wonderful	すてき (な)	one-piece dress	ワンピース
Nicole Kidman	ニコルキッドマン	only	だけ
night-time stalls	よみせ	open	あけます
nine	ここのつ、九つ	orange	オレンジ (の)
noisy	うるさい	orientation	オリエンテーション
north	きた、北	origami	おりがみ
		outdoor bath	ろてんぶろ
		outside	そと、外
		over there (away from both the speaker and listener)	
			あそこ
		overcoat	コート
		overseas	かいがい、海外、がいこく、外国

P

pants (underwear)	パンツ
pants, trousers	ズボン
paper	かみ
paper screen door	しょうじ
park	こうえん
part-time high school	ていじせい、てい時せい
part-time job	アルバイト
pass by	とおります
peach-coloured	ももいろ（の）
pen	ペン
pencil	えんぴつ
pencil case	ふでばこ
people	ひとびと、人々
period	〜じかんめ、〜時間目
period drama/film	じだいげき、時だいげき
period of 3 months	さんかげつかん、三か月間
period of time	かん、間
personal assistant	ひしょ
personal development	ほけん
personal history form	りれきしょ、りれき書
petrol station	ガソリンスタンド
pharmacist	やくざいし
pharmacy	くすりや
photo	しゃしん
photographer/camera operator	カメラマン
physical education	たいいく
pick up	むかえに行きます
picture	え
piercing, earrings	ピアス
pilot	パイロット
ping-pong/table tennis	ピンポン
pink	ピンク（の）
place	ばしょ
place	のせます
place (e.g. The 11th place)	い
place of residency	ほんせき、本せき
platform	ホーム
play	あそびます
play a game	ゲームします。
play a musical instrument (stringed or keyboard)	ひきます
Please come and play.	あそびに　きてください。あそびに　来てください。
Please come.	きてください。
Pleased to meet you.	どうぞよろしくおねがいします。
Please give me a hand.	てつだってください、手つだってください。
Please remember me.	よろしくおねがいします。
Please repeat it.	もういちどいってください。もう一ど言ってください。
Please send me a letter.	てがみを　ください。

Please speak more slowly.	ゆっくり言ってください。
Please take care.	きをつけてください。
Please try/do your best.	がんばってください
Please wait a moment.	しょうしょうおまちください、少々おまちください。
Please write back soon.	はやく　おへんじを　かいてください。はやく　おへんじを　書いてください。
pm	ごご
police officer	けいさつかん、けいかん
politician	せいじか、せいじ家
politics	せいじ
poor, pitiful	かわいそう
popular	にんきがあります、人気があります
population	じんこう、人口
port town	みなとまち、みなと町
postcard	はがき
post office	ゆうびんきょく
poster	ポスター
practise	れんしゅうします
prepare	じゅんびします
prettily	きれいに
pretty, clean	きれい（な）
primary school	しょうがく、小学
primary school/junior school	しょうがっこう、小学校
print	いんさつします
private	しりつ、私りつ
private school	しりつがっこう、私りつ学校
probably, don't you think?	〜でしょう
profile	プロフィール
protect	まもります
public	こうりつ
publishing company	しゅっぱんしゃ、出版社
pulling chopsticks	よせばし
pulsating heat from the sun	ぎらぎら
purple	むらさき（の）
push	おします
put on (additional clothing)	します
put on (hats)	かぶります
put on (top half or general clothing)	きます
put out	だします、出します
pyjamas	パジャマ

Q

question	しつもん
quickly	はやく
quiet	しずか（な）
quit	やめます

R

radio	ラジオ
rain	あめ
rainy season	つゆ
raw	なま、生
raw fish	なまの　さかな、生の　さかな
read	よみます、読みます
reading	どくしょ、読書
reading and writing	よみかた、読みかた
Really?	えー。
Really?	ほんとうですか。
reason for applying	しぼうのどうき
received	もらいました
record	ろくおんします
red	あか（い）
register, cashier	レジ
relax	リラックスします
remember	おぼえます
report	レポート
request/desire	きぼう
retired.	いんたいしています。
return	もどします、もどります、かえります
ribbon	リボン
rice cake	おにぎり
ride	のります
right	みぎ、右
right eye	みぎめ、右目
right hand	みぎて、右手
right-hand side	みぎがわ、右がわ
ring	ゆびわ
rise	あがります
rise	かわ、川
river	かわ、川
rock band	ロックバンド
rock concert	ロックコンサート
roll	まきます
rollerblading	ローラーブレード
rough, violent	らんぼう（な）
round	まるい
RSVP by Friday	へんじはきんようびまで。へんじは金曜日まで。
rubbish	ごみ
rubbish bin	ごみばこ
rude	しつれい（な）
ruler	ものさし

rules	きそく
run	はしります

S

sad, lonely, I miss her/him.	さびしい
salt	しお
sandals	サンダル
Sannen Hill	さんねんざか、三年坂
Sapporo	さっぽろ
sashimi	さしみ
say	いいます、言います
scary	こわい
scenery	けしき
school	がっこう、学校
school history	がくれき、学れき
school rules	こうそく、校そく
school yard	こうてい、校てい
science	かがく、か学
science fiction	エスエフ（SF）
score	スコア
sea	うみ
seasons	きせつ
seaweed	のり
second	ふたつめ、二つ目
second floor (first floor in Australia)	にかい、二かい
See you later.	じゃあ、またね。
see, watch, look	みます、見ます
seems sad	さびしそう。
self-introduction	じこしょうかい、自こしょうかい
Send me an e-mail.	Eメールしてね。
senior high school	こうこう、高校
serious	まじめ（な）
seven	ななつ、七つ
shaved ice treat	かきごおり
shirt	シャツ
shivering	ぶるぶる
shoe shop	くつや
shoe box	げたばこ、くつばこ
shoes	くつ
shop assistant	てんいん
shops	みせ
short	せが　ひくい、みじかい
shorts	はんズボン、半ズボン
short-sleeved shirt	はんそでシャツ、半そでシャツ
shoulder	かた
show	みせます、見せます
Showa reign (used for giving dates)	しょうわ
Shrek	シュレック
shrine	じんじゃ、じん社
side	がわ

side path/road	よこのみち	spouse	はいぐうしゃ
sign language	しゅわ、手話	spring	はる、春
silence	シーン	spring wind	はるかぜ、春かぜ
silly	ばか	sprinkling rain	しとしと
sing	うたいます	stabbing chopsticks	さしばし
singer	かしゅ、か手	stairs	かいだん
singing show	うたばんぐみ	stand up, to pass time	たちます
sit	すわります	Star Festival	たなばた
six	むっつ、六つ	stars	ほし
skateboard	スケートボード	start	スタート
sketch	したがき、下書き	start (I start)	はじめます
skilful at	とくい（な）	start (it starts)	はじまります
skinny, thin	ほそい	station	えき
skirt	スカート	steak	ステーキ
sleep	ねます	stomach	おなか
slowly	ゆっくり	stop	とまります
small	ちいさい、小さい	stormy	あらし
SMAP (a Japanese musical group)		story	はなし、話
	SMAP・スマップ	straight	まっすぐ
smile radiantly, beaming		strange	へん（な）
	にこにこする	street, road	みち
snack	おやつ	strict	きびしい
sneakers, runners	スニーカー	strong	つよい
snow	ゆき	strong wind	びゅーびゅー
snowman	ゆきだるま	strong wind in early spring	
so so	まあまあ		はるいちばん、春一ばん
soapie	ひるメロ	student	せいと、生と
sob, whimper	めそめそする	study	べんきょうします
society	しゃかい、社会	stuffed toy	ぬいぐるみ
sociology	しゃかいがく、社会学	subject	かもく
socks	くつした	subtitles	じまく
soft and soggy	ぐちゃぐちゃ	subway	ちかてつ、ち下てつ
something	なにか、何か	sugar	さとう
sometimes	ときどき、時々	sugoroku (a Japanese variety of parcheesi)	
song	うた		すごろく
soon	もうすぐ	suit	スーツ
sopping wet, soaking through		summer	なつ、夏
	びしょびしょ	summer holiday	なつやすみ、夏休み
sound of laughing	ワハハ	sumo	すもう
sounds of the big gong	かねのおと	sumo stable/school	すもうべや
south	みなみ、南	sumo wrestler	りきし
south-east	なんとう、南東	supermarket	スーパー
south-west	なんせい、南西	sushi mat	まきす
southern entrance	みなみぐち、南口	sweater, jumper	セーター
souvenir	おみやげ	sweating	たらたら
soy sauce	しょうゆ	sweets	おかし
spacious	ひろい	swim	およぎます
speak	はなします、話します	swimming pool	プール
speak fluently	ぺらぺらはなす、ぺらぺら話す		
special requests for the position			
	ほんにんきぼうきにゅうらん		
sports day	うんどうかい		
sports instructor	スポーツインストラクター		

T

table	テーブル
take	とります
take (a shower)	あびます
Take care of yourself.	おからだに　きを　つけて。
take off clothing	ぬぎます
take time, to cost money	かかります
talk	はなします、話します
tall	せが　たかい
Tama River	たまがわ、たま川
tank top	タンクトップ
tatami	たたみ
tatami room	たたみのへや
tatami room (traditional style)	わしつ
taxi driver	タクシーのうんてんしゅ、タクシーのうんてん手
taxi stand	タクシーのりば
tea cup/bowl	おちゃわん
tea party	ティーパーティー
teach/tell	おしえます
teacher	きょうし
teacher	せんせい、先生
technology	テクノロジー
telephone	でんわします、電話します
television	テレビ
television station	テレビきょく
ten	とお、十
Thank you for waiting.	おまたせ　しました。
Thank you very much.	どうもありがとうございました。
that ...	その
that one	それ
that one over there	あれ
that over there	あの
the first day	いちにちめ、1日目、一日目
the other day	せんじつ、先日
there (near the listener)	そこ
therefore	だから
thin, slim, skinny	やせている、ほそい
things to bring	もってくるもの、もって来るもの
think	おもいます／かんがえます
third	みっか、三日
this	この
this month	こんげつ、今月
this one	これ
this week	こんしゅう、今週
this year	ことし、今年
thongs	ぞうり
three	みっつ、三つ
tidal wave	つなみ
tie	ネクタイ
timetable	じかんわり、時間わり
tired	つかれます、つかれています
to be, to have, there is (for animals and people)	います
to become fat	ふとります
today	きょう、今日
together	いっしょに
toilet	おてあらい、お手あらい、トイレ
Tokyo	とうきょう、東京
tomorrow	あした
tonight	こんばん、今ばん、こんや、今や
too expensive	たかすぎます、高すぎます
touch	さわります
tour guide	ツアーガイド
tourist	かんこうきゃく
towards	ほう
towel	タオル
tower	タワー
town, city	まち、町
traditional	でんとうてきな
traffic lights	しんごう
train	でんしゃ、電車
travel	りょこうします、りょ行します
travel agent	りょこうがいしゃ、りょ行会社
trousers	ズボン
try	ためします
try hard	がんばります
T-shirt	Tシャツ
tsunami/tidal wave	つなみ
tummy, stomach	おなか
tuna	まぐろ
turn	まがります
turn off	けします
turn on	つけます
tutor	かていきょうし
TV or radio programme	ばんぐみ
two	ふたつ、二つ
typhoon	たいふう

U

udon noodles	うどん
Umeda Park	うめだこうえん
umm	えーと、ええと
unattractive, unfriendly	かっこわるい
uncle (humble term)	おじ
uncle (someone else's)	おじさん
understand	わかります、分かります
uniform	せいふく
university	だいがく、大学
university student	だいがくせい、大学生
until	まで
us (boys and men)	ぼくたち
use	つかいます

V

variety show	バラエティーショー
various	いろいろ（な）
very	とても
veterinarian	じゅうい
vinegar	す
visible, I can see ...	みえます、見えます
visual arts	びじゅつ
volcano	かざん、火山

W

wait	まちます
waitress	ウエイトレス
wake up	おきます
wall	かべ
wandering chopsticks	まよい　ばし
want to become	なりたい
warm	あたたかい
was nervous	きんちょうしました
was often attracted by	（〜に）よくあこがれました
wasabi	わさび
wash	あらいます
watch	とけい、時けい
waterski	すいじょうスキー、水上スキー
way of moving	うごかしかた
way of writing	よみかた、読みかた
way of holding	もちかた
we	わたしたち、私たち
wear (top half or general clothing)	きます
wear a hat	ぼうしをかぶります
wear glasses	めがねをかけます
wear make-up	けしょうします
wear sunglasses	サングラスをかけます
wear, put on (for additional clothing)	つけます
wear/put on (bottom half of clothing)	はきます
wearing (for additional clothing)	つけています
wearing (glasses)	かけています
weather	てんき
weather forecast	てんきよほう
week	しゅう、週
weekend	しゅうまつ、週まつ
weeping, sobbing	シクシク
weight	たいじゅう
Welcome home.	おかえりなさい。
Welcome/May I help you?	いらっしゃいませ
west entrance	にしぐち、西口
Western food	ようしょく、よう食
Western music	ようがく

Western-style room	ようしつ
what	なに、なん、何
What day of the week?	なんようび、何曜日
What kind of things?	どんな　もの
What kind of?	どんな
What month, what date?	なんがつなんにち、何月何日
What temperature?	なんど、何ど
What time?	なんじ、何時
What?	あれー。
What?	なにを、何を
wheelchair	くるまいす、車いす
when (you are) in trouble	こまったとき
when I was a child	こどものとき、子どもの時
When you do that	そうすると
Where?	どこで
Which?	どの
Which one?	どちらが、どれが
white	しろ（い）
Who?	だれが
Who with?	だれと
Why?	どうして、なぜ
Will you go home?	かえりますか。
win	かちます
wind	かぜ
windcheater/jumper	トレーナー
window	まど
windy	かぜが　つよい
winter	ふゆ、冬
winter season	とうき、冬き
with all one's might	いっしょうけんめい
woman	おんなのひと、女の人
Won't you come and play.	あそびに　きませんか。あそびに　来ませんか。
wonderful	すばらしい
word	ことば
work	しごと
work	はたらきます
work desk	しごとづくえ
work history	しょくれき
Wow!	わあー。
Wow! (casual)	へえ！
wrist	てくび、手くび
write	かきます、書きます
write fluently	すらすらかく、すらすら書く
Write me a reply!	へんじかいてね、へんじ書いてね。

Y

yakitori	やきとり
Yamaguchi (surname)	やまぐち、山口

Yasaka Shrine	やさかじんじゃ、やさかじん社
year by year	ねんねん、年々
year level	〜ねんせい、〜年生
yellow	きいろ（い）
yen	えん、円
Yes.	はい。
Yes. (casual)	うん。
Yes, go on.	はい、はい。
yesterday	きのう
you	あなた
You must come!	ぜひ きてね。ぜひ 来てね。
You're welcome.	どういたしまして。
young	わかい
younger brother (humble term)	
	おとうと
younger brother (someone else's)	
	おとうとさん
younger sister (humble term)	
	いもうと
younger sister (someone else's)	
	いもうとさん

Z

zero degrees	れいど
zoo	どうぶつえん

二百

NOTES

Kana-chan game

Inside the back cover of the Obento Supreme Student Book is a CD-ROM containing Kana-chan — a fun game that helps you learn hiragana. In the game, you must help Kana-chan find hidden hiragana characters before she runs out of time.

The Kana-chan game is available on the attached CD-ROM or can be downloaded from the Obento website (www.obento.com.au). It can be played on your mobile phone or personal computer. For instructions on how to download Kana-chan, see below.

Launching on your PC or Mac

Navigate to the CD-ROM and open either the 'Mac' or 'Win' folder. Mac users should double-click on the file named 'Kana' and Windows® users on 'Kana.exe'. You may require the free Adobe® Flash® Player software to view the game. Download Flash Player from www.adobe.com/products/flashplayer.

Launching on your mobile phone

You will first need to copy the game file 'Kana.swf' from the CD-ROM to your Macromedia® Flash Lite™-enabled mobile phone. Your mobile must support Flash Lite™ v2 or later. (There's a list of supported phones at www.adobe.com/mobile/supported_devices/handsets.html).

If you need to purchase 'Flash Lite™ 2 player', go to www.tinyurl.com/p8nwl.

Windows®: copying the Kana-chan game to your phone via USB

Ensure that you have installed the software that was supplied with your mobile phone on to your computer. Once installed, the software will enable you to transfer files from your computer to your Flash-enabled mobile phone.

For instance, with some Nokia mobile phones, you would install the 'Nokia Phone Browser', which is part of the 'Nokia PC Suite' software which can be found on the CD-ROM supplied with the phone.

Once the software is installed, you can copy files or folders from PC to your Nokia phone using the supplied USB cable.

To transfer the Kana-chan game to your mobile phone (a Nokia phone, in this example), use the following steps:

Launch 'Nokia PC Suite' (Start > Programs > Nokia PC Suite > Nokia PC Suite), then click on 'File manager'. This will launch the 'Nokia Phone Browser'. Use this browser to navigate to the CD-ROM containing the Kana-chan game. Locate the file 'kana.swf' (in the 'Mobile phone' folder).

Right click on the file and choose 'Copy'. Then, navigate to your mobile phone, and choose a location (e.g. 'memory card'), right click and choose 'paste'. 'Kana.swf' should then appear on your mobile phone. You can now quit out of the 'Nokia Phone Browser' software, and un-plug the phone from the computer.

To access the game, go to the phone's menu, select 'Flash', navigate to the memory card, click on 'Kana.swf' and then launch the file to play the game.

Alternatively, if your computer supports 'Bluetooth' wireless connectivity you can connect to your phone via Bluetooth, then copy and paste 'Kana.swf' from the CD-ROM to your phone. Please refer to your computer's user manual for further information regarding Bluetooth.

Mac OS X: copying the Kana-chan game to your phone via Bluetooth

The USB cable supplied with some phones, such as the Nokia 6680, are not compatible with Mac OS X.

However, if both your Mac and mobile phone support 'Bluetooth' wireless connectivity, you can transfer the 'Kana-chan' game file ('Kana.swf') from your Mac to your phone.

Ensure your phone's 'Bluetooth' connectivity is switched on. Then activate your Mac's Bluetooth (System Preferences > Bluetooth, then click on the 'Settings' button and click 'Turn Bluetooth On').

In the same Bluetooth window, now click on the 'Devices' button and click 'Set Up New Device'. Follow the on-screen prompts. Your Mac will scan for Bluetooth-enabled devices in your vicinity. Click on your phone name which appears listed in a window, and click 'Continue'. You will be prompted with a serial number on-screen. Enter this number on your phone's keypad to validate the Mac-phone connection.

Ensure that 'Bluetooth File Exchange' and 'Bluetooth File Transfer' are checked (ticked) under the 'Sharing' button.

Launch 'Bluetooth File Exchange' (Applications > Utilities). Choose File > 'Browse Device'. You should then see your phone listed in the window that appears. Select (highlight) your phone from the list, and click 'Browse'. Then click 'Send' in the new window that appears. Navigate and select the 'Kana.swf' file on the CD-ROM (in 'Mobile phone' folder) and click 'Send'.

You mobile phone will probably sound a tone when it receives the file via 'Bluetooth'. You may be asked if you want to accept the message. If you accept, the item is placed in the inbox folder of your phone's messaging facility. Open the message in the Inbox, select 'Kana.swf' and click 'Enter'. 'Kana.swf' will then open in the phone's Flash player.

On some phones you can now use the left soft key to access the Flash Lite menu.

In these options you can choose to copy the file to the memory card.